THE SPIRITUAL
PILGRAMAGE
AND PERILS
OF A REAL SOUTHERN
BABY BOOMER

THE SPIRITUAL PILGRAMAGE AND PERILS OF A REAL SOUTHERN BABY BOOMER

BY DONALD R. WATKINS

XULON PRESS

Xulon Press
2301 Lucien Way #415
Maitland, FL 32751
407.339.4217
www.xulonpress.com

© 2022 by D.R. Watkins

Paperback ISBN-13: 978-1-6628-4807-0
Ebook ISBN-13: 978-1-6628-4808-7

I dedicate this book to those that have grown up in dysfunctional families Linked to alcohol and severe depression developing into mental issues and those in those families that have denial issues. (Hide the family secrets) I also dedicate this book to those in the ministry struggling to do God's will in the battle for the souls of men having to fight the so-called religious leaders just like Jesus did over their nonsense rules, politics and condemnation of others.

Finally, I dedicate this book to my family that had to face the battles with me, especially my wife, Kathy, children, Stephanie, Lani, Ricky and grandchildren, Devan, Connor, Reace, Ryson, and Ryxon.

Table of Contents

INTRODUCTION

I t is my desire that when you read this book, focus on how God has moved and directed my life and in the lives of those around me. Very few times will I mention the full names of those that impacted my life, I had rather focus the attention on the spiritual aspects of my life.

I would also ask you not to make judgments until you read the entire book. Many lives have those negative events as well as positive events that would mold and make them what they are today.

If by chance you find similar experiences in your life, I pray that you would notice how God, through his word, molded and shaped a sinner like me, to follow and depend on him for everything. It was a long road all the good/bad/ugly where those events in due time would strengthen me like a body builder working with weights, my soul would work through a mass of negative experiences to strengthen my character and faith. Life is a battle with victories as well as defeats.

The battles within me were dealing with anger and trust issues that developed from childhood, well into adulthood. As I write this book, I am in my mid-seventies. Like the saying goes, I have been through everything. I might not remember too many details but I write what I remembered from my perspective from a young child into an adult.

There is nothing new under the sun. Ecclesiastes 1:9 (NIV)

If you are a servant of God, you will have a handful of friends you can trust. A well-known celebrity friend once told me that if you can count your true friends on one hand, you are blessed.

You could not imagine the struggles ministers go through, demands from denominations, church politics, family, and those that would want to discredit you in every way.

You have no enemies, you say? Alas, my friend, the boast is poor. He who has mingled in the fray of duty that the brave endure, must have made foes. If you have none, small is the work that you have done. You've hit no traitor on the hip. You've dashed no cup from perjured lip. You've never turned the wrong to right. You've been a coward in the fight. Charles Mackay (Charles Mackay was a Scottish poet, journalist, author, anthologist, novelist, and songwriter, remembered mainly for his book Extraordinary Popular Delusions and the Madness of Crowds. *Source:* https://quotepark.com/authors/charles-mackay/

John 16: 33 (NIV) These things I have spoken to you, that in Me you may have peace. In the world you will have tribulation; but be of good cheer, I have overcome the world."

God can do anything in your life to improve and make changes it; it just takes time and faith. He will follow through in His timing.

As I write this book, the sequence of events is not in order, over seventy-five years, time and sequences can get jumbled. Focus on the events and not the time line. It is my prayer that you will be blessed and encouraged!

I dedicate this book to my family that had to face the battles with me, especially my wife, Kathy, children, Stephanie, Lani, Ricky and grandchildren, Devan, Connor, Reace, Ryson, and Ryxon.

STARTING OFF

My father was born in 1915. His father owned a grocery store and had a construction business. As dad grew, he worked in both. Dad never gave me details of his early life, but he did tell me some horror stories that I will not mention. In those days there were family secrets that you just didn't talk about. I think some on dad's side know some of those secrets.

In dad's teens, he was somewhat on the wild side, dad and his friends were in a motorcycle club. (Not like gangs of today) He continued to work for his father, especially in building construction. That experience of construction and contracting would forge a bright financial future for him.

When WWII broke out. Dad at that time was a contractor for the government building military bases in Colorado and later in California. While doing contract work in California he stayed in Hollywood; even making some friends with some of the celebrities.

If you were to look at old photos of him during that time, you might have thought of him as one of the stars. He told me many years later that people would stop him and ask for an autograph. He was dark complected. I was told, some thought he looked like Errol Flynn with that dark wavy hair and thin mustache.

Life in Hollywood was cut short when Dad got a letter from his father that the draft board was looking for him. He thought because he worked for the US government and was already into his thirties, he was exempt. His dad stated that they had a warrant out for his arrest.

Immediately dad went to a recruiting office and signed up in the US Army. With his experience in construction, he thought he would wind up in an engineering unit. That never happened, after bootcamp he was assigned to an infantry unit. Due to his age and leadership, in a very short time he became a master sergeant. My father was with the 70th Infantry Division in France. His particular unit experienced 85 straight days of constant combat, night and day. He almost was killed when a sniper's bullet went through the window of his jeep just inches from his head.

Dad came home from France at the end of WWII and was stationed in Virginia until his release from the military. From then he worked a short time for the government securing farm loans for veterans.

Born in 1920, mom came from a large family. In the area of Nickelsville Georgia a small rural community in the northwest part of the state. This southern community exemplifies a typical rural community in the South. The Smith/Middleton families worked farms growing things like corn, cotton and vegetables. With such a large family most of the veggies went to feeding the family.

Emory Smith, mom's dad was skilled as a blacksmith and grist miller, (grain grinder for corn meal), he also was skilled in working with copper – (moonshine stills). Granny, Sally Kerr, Smith was a fantastic quilt maker and could cook anything on a cast iron-potbelly wood burning stove. Mom once told me that family and neighbors, would help in working the fields during harvest times picking cotton and corn ears.

When WWII broke out, my mother along with other women in the area, went to work at the Lockheed plant in Marietta Georgia, a real-life Rosie riveter. She and others would commute by train, 50 miles (sometimes by bus).

Mom was proud to work on bombers and fighter planes, her favorite plane was the P38. The workers would stay a few days getting rest and sleep when they could. At times the workers would go back to their homes for a short stay then back to work. Mom's family in Nicklesville worked the farms, the government considered that essential and yet several of mom's siblings enlisted in the military. The Smith family was recognized by the state of Georgia as having five family members serving in the military at that time.

My favorite uncle, J.L., was married to mom's sister he lived in Dalton. My father and Uncle were best of friends. Dad came home of leave before going to Europe. J.L. introduced him to Mom. Immediately they had developed an attraction for each other. At that time dad was stationed in Missouri. There, he called mom to come and visit him. They were married there on base.

Both of my parents have deep roots in the foothills of the Georgia mountains that go back before the American Revolution. Our family's bloodlines include Scot/Irish and Cherokee.

I was born in Dalton Georgia, a small industrial town in the northwest part of Georgia, qualifying me to be a true

Southerner. As the saying goes, "American by birth, Southern by the grace of God."

My birth was shortly after WWII in Europe was over qualifying me to be a true baby boomer along with the other two and a half million, that were born right after the war and the thousands that were born after the Korean conflict.

There were many relatives on both mom and dad's sides of the family. Both my dad and mother had been married before the war and both of them had a daughter. The daughter my mother had was the one I grew up with, while my other sister dad had, I never knew I had until years later when she and her family came to visit. That was a shocker to me because I was never told about dad's daughter until they came to visit. I had not known that they had been divorced previously until I was in about the 5th grade in school.

I think I was about three years of age, maybe four, when my family moved from Dalton down to Cartersville. It was there where faint memories kick in of the simple life of living in a small town. It was also where my spiritual pilgrimage would begin as I contemplated the fact there was a God that existed.

Cartersville, is about an hour's drive North from downtown Atlanta. In Cartersville there were textile mills, a tire plant and plenty of cotton fields all around that community. I remember an underwear factory with the brand name –(EZ-Underwear) If you lived within the city limits, everything was in walking distance. It is what you might see on a television show about life in a small rural community. Slow quiet and peaceful describes this town rich in historical events.

Every town from Atlanta to Chattanooga had a rail line running north and south. There was also Highway 41 (Old Dixie Highway) that started up north in Illinois and ran all the way down to Florida. Both the rail lines and highway 41 would go through the middle of each town in North Georgia into Atlanta and on. These transportation routes that ran through the center of each town providing transportation and goods to each community.

Up until the early 19th century, everything north of Atlanta into Tennessee was Cherokee land, until they found gold on the land. The Georgia militia moved the Cherokees out to Oklahoma – (Tails of Tears).

Many Cherokees hid in the mountains and came back to live in the same area they once lived in after the Civil war. Nicklesville Georgia had been Cherokee land. Both mom and dad's family had Cherokee blood.

Cartersville had many Cherokee people living there, some of the friends I had in the neighborhood I lived, were of pure Cherokee blood. Many in the Jim Crow south were subjected to racial discrimination.

My family moved into a duplex with a couple that owned the house. This family would become life-long friends with my family. Bill and Coreen their names would be etched in my heart forever. They were like a second set of parents.

While both mom and dad worked, much of the time I had to have a babysitter. Coreen watched me from time to time. When she worked, my parents would hire a black lady to sit with me.

The duplex set on a bluff facing a junction of two main roads leading into town. The duplex supported a long-covered porch elevated, that faced the road. There were some chairs. With a child's imagination the porch had been a great place to play and it was safe. It felt like a towering building, you looked down at everything.

Sometimes peaceful quiet moments came just sitting in the chairs and counting the cars and trucks that passed by followed by moments of absolute stillness meshed with tranquility.

That was going to change. Technology was advancing rapidly after the war. A television station from Atlanta had begun broadcasting several hours during the day from mid-afternoon into early evening.

Soon, the excitement of television came to us when Dad had bought a television set. It was a small wooden boxy thing with a screen so small that you had to be close to the screen that only 3 or 4 could watch it at a time. Dad had to change tubes from time to time, they kept burning out. My all-time favorite was Howdy Doody.

Though through the years, we had many television sets. Dad kept that first set for over 17 years. I guess that first set was very special to dad. He gave it up when he could no longer find tubes for it.

Those were good times I recall in the dim pictures of a four-year-old boy's memory. Over the years Coreen, my sitter and next-door neighbor would remind me of the wonderful days. I am glad that through the years that Coreen would remind of those events each time I would visit, well into my adulthood.

Bill, her husband was a die-hard Republican and a casket salesman. The year that Eisenhower ran for president, I walked with Bill up and down the streets handing out the "I like Ike buttons." I wish I had kept one.

Next door to the duplex was an old house that looked more like a farm. (At that time there were no zone restrictions) The couple that lived there, raised chickens and sold eggs and chickens as a source of income.

They also had grandkids that would come over to visit. That was fun due to the fact one kid was my age, giving me the opportunity to be with those like me playing for hours on end.

One day one of the kids came to get my sister and I. Something was happening. As we went over with my sister to see what was going, we saw a most unusual site – There in the fenced yard was a rooster running around without a head. It is a fact that chickens can and do run around with their heads cut off. Later when I was older, I learned that when rosters stopped doing their job being a rooster, they were replaced and eaten in a stew because the meat was tough.

Shortly, after that experience, my first spiritual encounter happened with Coreen. This encounter happened when the old man with the chickens next door had died. Because both my parents worked and my sister was in school, I had to stay with my sitter, Coreen.

As it was customed in that day, when someone died, they would have displayed the body in a casket or on a table in the home of the deceased. That was called *Sittin' up with the dead*. My baby sitter, Coreen took me with her when she visited the family next door to take them food; a custom which in the South is still practiced.

There in the large living room was the body of the old man wearing an old suit that smelled like a dusty rug. I was scared out of my wits. As we walked back to the duplex, I began to cry with fear thinking that death was a frightening thing to consider for a young lad.

Back at the duplex Coreen sat me down. "Rick, do you remember when I would go next door to get some eggs from those chickens?" I responded, "Yes, I remember!"

Coreen reminded me of how I had watched chicks hatch from the farm next door. I remember when the chick came out, the shell was left behind. Coreen told me that was the same thing I saw next door. "He is not there anymore, that body was his shell. He has gone to be with God." Coreen lovingly explained.

That was the first time I began to think about God, but it would be many years before I would have a personal relationship with him through Christ. However, this was the moment that I began a spiritual pilgrimage of knowing there is a God, Father and creator of all things.

Across the road from the duplex was another family that would be life-long friends with my family. Jack and Ann Nealy and their two daughters, Pat and Penny. My parents had known them when they all lived in Dalton Ga.

Like Coreen and Bill, the Nealy family would be significant figures. In our lives. Mom and Ann were the best of friends. Years later the bonding with the Nealy family would grow in another location far from Cartersville. The Nealy family would be a part of my life for over 60 years.

A day came when we would move into our first house. The house was outside the city limits south of Cartersville and close to the Etowah Indian Mounds, a historic site where native Americans once thrived next to the Etowah River. The mounds were built by the native Americans and still remain there today.

The mounds were a favorite playground for the local kids in those days. I remember spring and summertime; all kinds of flowers would be blooming on the mounds. The favorite of all these was the Honeysuckle flowers. If you held the flowers and pulled the bottom of the stem, sweet honeylike liquid would come out for you to suck on. You had to be careful you, were competing with the bees.

The neighborhood kids could play anywhere except going close to the Etowah River and a sink hole close to where we lived. The river was scary because the current was fast with summer rains. The sink hole was safe but deep. No one went swimming in it there were rumors that is where the used to throw unknown dead bodies. I think they said that to keep kids away.

Today, there is a museum when at one time those mounds were covered with weeds and bushes and was an ideal place to play. Now you have to pay a fee to see the mounds that are now kept pristine. The sink hole was filled and became a small pond.

I don't think we stayed there long because my family once again made another move to a small community south of Cartersville, Emerson Georgia. It was there another spiritual event happened.

From time to time, the family would attend a Baptist church there; including, vacation bible school. That was my first experience in a church. The church was old and when grown-ups walked on those old wooden floors, it made all kinds of squeaks and groans. Lighting seemed to be dim for a church. It was very loud when trains came through, the church was located near the tracts.

Our home was up on a hill straight up from the church. We could see all of Emerson, the train tracks and the top of the courthouse in Cartersville. I visited there a few years back, with trees grown you could not get the same view.

It was nice and quiet in Emerson except when trains came by blowing their whistles. I would love hearing those trains whistles and the sounds of the locomotives.

As dad and mom advanced their work careers making more money, we moved back into Cartersville's city limits. We moved into a house on Maybelle Street. At the end of the street was a large cotton field in which all the neighborhood children would play.

There were a whole flock of kids there, I can remember. However, there was one kid, Billy, that was my age. I think by that time we were about the age of five or six. Because our parents knew each other, we had become good friends.

One day I went to Billy's house while his mother and mine went out shopping for a short time a couple of blocks away in town. Billy wanted to show me something special he found in his dad's bedroom.

There, he showed me a deck of playing cards and on the cards were photos of naked girls. I got so scared! I thought if anyone caught us there, we would be whipped and wind up in jail. I carried that guilt a long time, even when I got older and similar events happened.

That summer I went to another Vacation Bible School. Lord help me Jesus – I don't want to go to jail

Vacation Bible school was the norm for kids in the south during summer. Although many would ignore going to Sunday school after thanksgiving for fear of winding up in a Christmas program that often made them look silly in bath robes, towels with rags on their heads and around their waist.

The last summer on Maybelle Street Dad had bought a larger tv. During shows on Friday or Saturday evenings, he would put the tv in a window facing the back yard. Neighbors would come over; all would watch the shows while we kids played in the yard. The best and funniest show was called, Your Show of Shows, with Sis Caesar and Imogene Coca, Honeymooners and I love Lucy. There were many other shows, but I don't remember all of them.

While we lived there on Maybelle Street, Dad had bought some land on the westside of Cartersville and soon started construction of a new home. Our family was moving on up. On weekends we would go to the house under construction. My job was to sweep and pick up rubbish.

Dad did a lot of construction work; before WWII that is what he did for the federal government before he got drafted.

Soon after the construction of our new home was started, I was enrolled in the first grade at Cherokee Elementary school. The school was just one block down from the house Dad was building for us.

Back then, they did not have something like public pre-school and kindergartens, they were private and costly. For most kids like myself, first grade was your first school experience.

The first day, in the first grade, with my first teacher, I got punished. Wanting to make friends, I thought by making them all laugh, I would make friends and be popular. All I did was pass gas very loudly from both ends, making the entire class-room roar with laughter and causing a couple of other kids to belch loudly.

Immediately the teacher told me never to do that again in the classroom, then she whacked my hand with a wooden ruler. It did not hurt that much, but I had to bite my lip from laughing. Inside my mind, I was laughing so hard I almost peed in my pants.

My use of humor would grow over the years. It was one of the avenues I used to cope with negative conditions at home, and to help me make friends. There was even a time later in life, I actually wanted to be a stand-up comedian. God had other plans for me.

Each grade in that school, we started with the pledge of allegiance and the Lord's prayer. Advancing to higher grades, the recitation of Psalms 100 was added with the singing of the national anthem.

There was a terrible negative event that happened to me. In the 6th grade. We were going to have a music teacher each Friday in the afternoon before school got out. This was something new and exciting, I love music. I had a deep desire to learn to play an instrument, maybe even to sing in a choir.

In class one day, the teacher asked if anyone knew what the musical scale was. Just that past Wednesday while watching the (original) Mickey Mouse club, the show was teaching the musical scale.

I raised my hand to answer the question, and sang as loud as I could – *doe ray me fa so la tee doe!* At that, the class roared with laughter. That teacher grabbed both my ears and walked me into the hall. "You will never be in my class again and I will make sure you will never be in music as long as you live."

It did come to pass; in school I was never allowed to take any kind of music. Years later on my school records it stated that I was musically incompetent and should never take any kind of musical class. Sad that one event an adult can alter the life of a child that way. That was back in the 1950's I think. Things like that have changed, I hope they have changed. I love music old gospel, rock and roll, and country.

EVERYTHING IS NEW

Slowly we moved into the new home. Everything was new and everything was ours. On the westside of the house was built a brick barbeque pit with a large wooden picnic table that was under a large wooden roof. A tall wooden fence surrounded the area. Over the years dad had a lot of parties. Remember, being young and in the first grade and everything was large. Years later as an adult driving by the old house looked much smaller. Only the trees looked larger.

This place would also become the play place for all the kids in the neighborhood. Our imaginations could be stretched with no limits. A couple of times the neighborhood kids put on skits we made up. It was like the tv show, Spanky and his gang. We all called that place the "Fort."

A few years later a Kid from a rich, well to do family lived up the hill. His folks had a large home and lot. His dad had built his son a small Fort in their yard that not only looked authentic, the fort had a guard house with a stairway. I did not mind all the kids, including me playing there. His fort was so real looking, who could resist?

It did not take long for me to get acquainted with the kids in the neighborhood. Strange fact, all of them had older sisters like me. Wes. Lewis and Bill.

These guys were my age that was great – but I always thought of Lewis as my best friend. Lewis was a Christian boy with a serious Christ-like value system. Truly, this impacted my life and set an example. One summer someone got polio. It was suggested all in town get shots of penicillin. In that day that is all they had; the polio vaccine would come later in time.

The television news would show pictures and films of people in iron lungs. That was very scary especially if you were claustrophobic.

I had never had a shot that I remembered and the thought it was scary. Lewis my friend and some others in the neighborhood went together. Many young kids were crying and scared of the shot.

I noticed when Lewis got his shot, he did not even flinch. I thought if he can do it so can I. That Christian boy had a powerful influence in my life. The next influence that Lewis would have, was taking dance lessons just a block up the street. Lewis and I would take tap dancing classes and would dance in a recital event at a local theater. It seemed that anything Lewis did, I wanted to do.

But there was one more person that I grew to respect and love, Hattie.

During those days, in the Jim Crow south, Black people lived within their own communities separated from white communities. Our new house was across the road of one of those black communities. There was even a small grocery store in the community. The neighborhood kids would sneak off to buy candy there. Many times, kids were sent to pick up milk or bread most white people stores were closed by 6.00pm.

One late afternoon when the sun was setting, I was about seven or eight years old, I heard the most beautiful music I had ever heard coming down and across the road. As I got closer, I saw an elderly black lady chopping wood while singing.

Drawing near to her, she stopped singing. "What are you doing little boy, don't you know you are not supposed to be over here." She shouted.

I asked," What kind of music is that, I have never heard that kind before and I like hearing it."

"That is good ole gospel singing boy, ain't you ever heard of that, do your folks know you're here."

I stayed fixated on the music, "What is Gospel music?"

"That singing about God and his son Jesus and the wonderful things he does for folks."

Being inquisitive I ask, "How come your chopping all that wood?"

She told me that she had a wood burning stove that she used for cooking and for heat in the winter. Her little cottage only had two rooms and an outhouse. As she showed me around her place she asked," Would you tell your folks I do house cleaning and sittin' with kids.

As I left her home, I had felt the presence of very nice lady. For the remaining years at our house, she was cleaning and sittin' with me. from time to time. I loved her, I felt love that she had flowing out all the time.

One sad day came, I would not see her anymore. She was up in years and she told me that her grandmother had been a slave until Sherman came through. She said many former slaves followed Sherman. Later. She told me her mother had died right after giving her birth. She never knew exactly how old she was, there were no record of her birth she told me one time. I don't know who raised her, maybe a relative.

Hattie seemed to disappear – I think now she probably passed and went home to be with Jesus. She was old though I do not know how old. I learned much from her on my spiritual pilgrimage.

One day, I heard Mom very upset, talking to Dad. The jest of the conversation was that due to the police action that was happening in Korea, the US Army was asking my dad to come back, especially due to his combat experience and leadership as a master sergeant.

In order to serve, Dad chose to enter the Air Force reserves in a supply unit located on a base just north of Atlanta – from time to time we would not see him especially on weekends. But he was safe during that conflict.

Later when I was much older, he would tell me the horrors of war as well as crazy things that happened to him. I cannot fathom that his unit had spent 85 days in a continuous battle in France, day and night so fighting went on 24/7 His unit was under constant attack from the Germans. He told me day and night, there was no break.

When they finally got a break, they were so tired, dad and his men slept on pews in a Catholic church that was partially bombed out. Dad said that they forgot what day of the week it was, it was Sunday.

It was common that soldiers killed in battle, their bodies would be placed in local churches on the pews until they could be picked up.

When the town's people started coming in to worship, the sound of the churches bell rang.

Waking the soldiers sleeping, when they suddenly stood up, the locals freaked and ran out into the street. Later, the towns people brought food and wine for dad and his unit.

Years later dad told me the unit owed much to the supply trucks bringing food, supplies and much needed ammo. These trucks were driven by black soldiers. Dad had a great respect for those men. Dad told me one time while driving in Florida," I don't think we would have survived without them keeping supplies coming in."

Dad had a great respect for black people. Later I found out, others did not have the same respect, which dad resented. I learned later that his great grandmother was part Cherokee and black, but I don't know how true that is. When I was about 8 or 9, I got my mouth washed out with soap for using the "N" word. A lot of white kids were using that word.

VISITING THE FAMILY AND THE FAMILY VISITING US.

While living in Cartersville, we would often spend time going back to Calhoun and Dalton to visit relatives. Because my parents came from large families, there was a whole bunch of cousins. One time I heard dad say that my sister and I had, at that time, about 47 cousins; both sides of the family included.

Visiting the Calhoun area was not bad especially if my cousin Gary was there, he was my age. The Calhoun area was all farms where mom's family lived. Most of the cousins on Mom's side were girls. The farms of mom's family were places of play and have adventures.

Calhoun was another railroad town. It was very small in those days and the buildings downtown there were very old. The old Dixie Highway 41 went right through the middle of the town.

Dalton was a much better place to visit and stay the night. Like Cartersville it was a small community in the foothills of North Georgia. Remembering the mountains in the east hid the sunrise, while the mountains in the west hid the sunset.

Like Cartersville, at night you hear the train whistles breaking the silence of the evening. Dalton's downtown was one long street that ran parallel to the rail road. Most all the stores in town were right on that main street.

My cousin Gary's dad, uncle Buddy, worked in one of the five and dime stores. Many times, on weekends Gary and I would go up and down the street. Uncle J.L. and aunt Maude worked at a store right next to Buddy's store.

In Dalton my favorite aunt Maude and Uncle, J.L. lived in a large old vintage home that was built before the Civil War. It was like a castle to a young boy such as myself. A perfect place to play and explore. One day while exploring all the nooks and crannies I discovered a wasp nest, that was not fun, being stung all over my arms and face.

While staying, I had fun, there, they had cats, a View Master (to look at slides of Hawaii) and play blocks and in that big house the food was great as well.!

In the winter a glowing hot fireplace warmed most of the home. In the summertime there was fried catfish, homemade ice cream and watermelon. I always looked forward to going there. Sometimes, I felt more at home from there than I did back in Cartersville.

In the early years my aunt Maude would take me to the First Baptist church of Dalton. At that time, she was a Sunday school teacher.

When routinely visited my dads' family. The church was very different it was a church of the Nazarene. Sunday school was fine and the worship service was always filled with people giving their testimonies of how Jesus had saved them or how they were healed by God.

Grandfather, Watkins was a very strong and faithful Christian man. For years he continued to point me to Jesus, year after year, even when I was a grown man.

While visiting the relatives when I was a bit older, I began to notice that many on both sides of the families distanced themselves from me. Many times, I would go outside and be by myself unless my cousin Gary was there. But of course, we would get ourselves into a lot of mischief especially if we were caught smoking rabbit tobacco. Rabbit tobacco was a weed that when the leaves were dried you could wrap it up in paper and smoke it. If you chewed the green leaves, it tasted horrible but when you spit, it had that brown-orange color just like real chewing tobacco.

Years later Grandfather Watkins would reveal to me the reason he thought the families ignored me. By that time, I had developed an internal battle with biter anger issues and acts of rage within me that increased down the road. Those negative qualities only increased down the road.

Several times during the year we had a couple of mother's brothers come and stay a few days. Truth of the matter they were drying out from long drunken binges. They would stay a few days getting sober and then leave to go back to their homes.

I did not understand why, until a painter came to paint one summer. I don't remember his name, in remembering him, I just called him, Joe.

Joe would come and paint and at lunch time he would sit on the stoop to eat, then he would light up a cigarette. I was fascinated (as a young boy) to see him blow smoke rings. He would ask me about my life and how I was doing. We were buddies!

One day Joe did not come to finish the job. I overheard my parents in our kitchen talking; Joe had been in jail and while he was there, he cut his throat with a knife and died. I was heartbroken. *Why?* I asked myself?

Days later, I ask Dad why Joe did that. Dad told me that after WWII, many soldiers had a difficult time adjusting back to a normal life and that their minds were filled with battle scenes of death and destruction as well as guilt of the things they had to do.

That, I believe that was the case for my mother's brothers that came to the house to dry out. They had both been in France on D-Day. I was told one of them had crashed in a glider and was the only survivor; It was days before they found him tangled in a German barbed wire field. I don't know about the other uncle.

We had more visitors from family while living in the new house. The big surprise came when dad told me my sister from Cleveland Ohio was coming to visit. "Do you mean I have two sisters?" Up until then I was not aware that both of my parents had been married before.

When they arrived the second surprise was my Cleveland sister had a daughter my age. Dad laughed and ask how does it feel to be an uncle to someone your own age? I didn't think it was funny at all. They didn't stay long. Over the years I only saw that sister about 5 or 6 different times.

Down town Cartersville was just a short walk away. Kids in a small town could roam just about anywhere on their own. The best thing for kids to do on Saturday, was watching cartoons on television in the morning. After cartoons if you had about 75 cents you could go to the afternoon matinee at the local movie theater. For just 75 cents, you got admission, a small bag of popcorn and a Coke. Before the main attraction movie, you had cartoons and a series each week. My favorite was Buck Rogers. Most all of the matinee movies were cowboy movies. Sometimes they had a Tarzan movie or the Three Stooges.

Over the years in Cartersville, we did not have many family members come and visit, but I sure had fun visiting Dalton and Calhoun. I had good memories of Dalton and the family that lived in that marvelous house. Summer time we would go to a local pool at the base of Rockface mountain. (Where a civil war battle took place.) Though I had learned to swim at a local lake, my swimming was perfected at Rocky face.

Visiting the Papaw Watkins's home was often boring unless the male cousins were there from Rome Georgia. My cousin's visits were short, they spent much more time with their dad's family at Mill Creek Gap.

In Dalton Dad had a special friend, Junior G. He and his family lived on the far west side of Dalton at the base of a place called Dug Gap. That was a fantastic place to be and play. I loved the rock formations near the top.

Junior G. had all girls; one was my age and we would play together. For years, she was much like a flesh and blood sister. We would watch TV or play games. The best fun was going up the mountain to Dug gap. I think we had a crush on each other. Sometime s you can tell these things when you look into some-one's eye. If not romantic, I know we were the best of friends. I had been told that dad and Junior G. had been friends as boys just like myself and Junior's daughter.

BAPTISM – VACATION BIBLE SCHOOL – CHURCH – AND A MIRACLE

`Lewis, was my best friend that lived right across the street. In that time, Lewis and his family were members of the First Baptist Church of Cartersville.

The church was famous due to the fact that it was where Lottie Moon began her ministry that led her to be a missionary to China. Lewis's father was a deacon there. Each year Baptist would raise money for missions in her name.

Many times, Lewis would have me come to church services, especially during communion, the Lord's Supper. Lewis told me they had real wine. We would sit in the back pew and sip a thimble sized glass of a very dry tasting wine.

One day Lewis's father asked me if I wanted to be baptized. I looked up at the baptistry that appeared to be two stories high above the pulpit, knowing that I had not learned to swim yet I said in a loud slow voice," NOOOOO THANNNNK YOOOOOU" His father chuckled and said, "Someday you will be, I just know it" I smiled at him as he walked us home.

It was not long after that as dad was promoted working for the City of Cartersville, it was proper for those in political power to attend Sam Jones Memorial Methodist church -right across the street from city hall. I think that dad wanted to go there because in the Baptist church they were against any kind of drinking of alcohol. (except for real wine at communion)

I occasionally remember from time to time; dad would bring a gallon of a clear liquid in a gallon jar. Then he would put dried peaches or apricots in the jar. In a short time. The color of the liquid would turn color looking like tea. People in the south would put tea bags in a similar jar and set it out in the sun making sun tea. People drinking moonshine would camouflage their shine making it look like sun tea.

When I was older, wanting some tea, opening the jar, an overwhelming smell of alcohol filled the room. Good thing, nobody was home. Getting in trouble meant some serious punishment with a belt or switch.

One evening the family got dressed, we were going to church in the middle of the week. I knew that the church did not have a Wednesday evening service. I ask. "Why are we going there?"

The response was, "We are all getting baptized!"

I am thinking to myself, *Then, why would they let me wear my best clothes. I don't think mom would like all of our clothes to get wet, and think of how the car seats* would feel. I still had the fear of the Baptist church just down the street and that baptistry up so high.

"Don't worry!" dad said," "At this church they sprinkle." As we walked into the large sanctuary with some dim lights at the altar, I thought to myself, "This is really spooky!"

We all got on our knees at the altar when the minister asked this question, "Do all of you declare your devotion to God and Christ Jesus His son and do you declare your faithfulness and devotion to the church?" We all said yes and a handkerchief was placed on top of our heads.

The minister came down the line of the family pouring a few drops of water on the hanky that was placed on top of our heads. Well, we attended that church as a family until we moved to Florida.

That summer I still wanted to go to the Baptist church for vacation Bible school, that is where my friend Lewis went. It was there I would experience my first miracle. A significant mark in my spiritual pilgrimage.

My friend, Lewis and I would walk to the church. It was only about four blocks from where we lived. My parents had very strict rules to go home right after vacation Bible school was over. One day I disobeyed. I think Lewis had to go somewhere with his mom, he was not with me that day.

That day our VBS lesson was on the story of Naman, the leper. The story is found in the Bible, 2nd Kings chapter 5. Naman was told that in order to get rid of his leprosy, he had to wash himself in the Jordan river seven times. At first, he didn't want to but later did it and was healed. I thought that was a neat story.

That was some story that stuck in my mind for years, God does manifest miracles in peoples' lives. Naman was not even a Jew. Would he do a miracle for me, not having been baptized? Later in life I would experience many more, miracles that would change people's lives. This day I was going to experience my first one.

VBS that day was over about 2:00 p.m. I was supposed to walk straight home. Well, as I was leaving the church, I noticed that the church was constructing a small playground.

There was a large sandbox that had just been painted. A sign warned, the paint was still wet. Remember, back then, there was no latex quick drying paint. There were some toys in the sand and I thought that I could ease over and play in the sand before I went home.

The sand box had great shade from large oak trees and when the sun came through the leaves it made sun spots on the sand. I had lost time playing there. Having heard the court house clock chime it was 3:00 pm I panicked. "I have to get home before mom or I am going to get it!'

Forgetting about the wet paint, I climbed out of the sand box my hands stuck to the wet dark evergreen colored paint. I ran home with the fear of getting a good whipping. At home, I went straight into the half bathroom located next to my bedroom, with some old rags at hand.

I thought to myself, *If it worked for Naman it will work for me.* I wash my hands six times, but the paint did not come. Crying with fear, I washed the seventh time, all the paint peeled off of my now waterlogged hands. I had experienced my first miracle. To me, waterlogged or not, it was a miracle. It had deepened my thoughts of God. I thought, "His stuff really works!" Just in time, immediately after that I heard mom drive up.

My spiritual pilgrimage was moving again! Thank you, God!

Perks and quirks

The Korean conflict was finally over, dad did not have to go down to Marietta anymore. The only time we went down that way was to do shopping in Atlanta and go to the Varsity, a hot dog place to get the best hot dogs and fries.

There were lots of celebrations that year because all thought that there would be no more wars. My parents had many parties outside in that fenced area. Even though at that time the county was a dry county, you could buy booze in one county and drink it in a dry county if you did not get caught.

As a young lad, mom had some quirks that I did not understand until years later. No laundry or cleaning on Sundays. That is the Lord's Day. She told me that was practiced when she grew up in Nicklesville. Even cooking most foods were done on Saturday.

The next thing was the daily weekdays of delivered milk that had to be de -creamed. The cream was on the top of the glass container in which she carefully skimmed off to use in coffee and cooking purposes.

The item I was involved in was the burning of paper trash. Paper was separated to be burned in a special wired basket. She did not want to pay for the extra garbage can pick-up. The last thing she and I did until my brother was old enough; on Halloween she would drive to the rich, well to do parts of the town to get better quality candy for the whole family

The most horrible thing that mom did, whenever we got sick and had to stay home from school, we had to take a large dose of castor oil. The taste was nasty, and it gave you diarrhea. If you refused to take it, you had to go to school.

HOLIDAYS – THE GOOD, THE BAD, THE UGLY

Holidays always meant going to Calhoun and Dalton in the same day or weekend. It was rare that we spent Christmases at home.In 1954 we had a new addition to our home; my brother had been born. I was never to get close to him, for some reason my parents had a guard of protection around him. It was like I had some kind of disease that would kill him. I would get a scolding or a slap if I bothered him in anyway. He was named after dad, Terry Earl. I don't know where the name Terry came from.

My brother took dad's name, I was named after his buddies that saved dad's life. I carry the names with pride. Donald, was a man from Wisconsin and Richart was a man from Wales in England.

One crazy thing happened one night with my brother and I. The room lights were out because it was easier to see the television. I was eating my favorite sandwich which was a sliced banana and mayonnaise sandwich with some cool aid to drink. The rest of the family was decorating the Christmas tree.

By that time my brother was a toddler and had started walking. I was watching Davy Crockett, a Disney show series at that time. While I was watching the show, my little brother, he toddled his way by me. I felt a banana slice fall from my sandwich and bent down to pick it up to put back in the sandwich.

When I bit down, I noticed the texture and flavor was not like what I was used to. Looking at my brother who was wearing a saggy cloth diaper with yellow stools falling out. WOW, I bit into one of those stools. I thew the sandwich away and continued watching Davy. I was only ten -years-old at the time and was not bothered by the thought I bit into my brother's stool.

The good Christmas times were spent in Dalton with my favorite aunt, uncle and sister/cousin Janice. That fireplace was terrific, the fully decorated tree filled with decorations, a house filled with love added to that the smell of food and treats. Those times were the best!

Another great Christmas time, the Dalton Tatum's came down to Cartersville. Being good Baptist, they wanted to attend the first Baptist of Cartersville on Christmas eve. After the service we went outside to see a light snow coming down. The lights from inside the church, lit the stained-glass windows enhanced a Christmas card picture in my mind. I can still feel the snowflakes on my face and hear the organ playing inside as folks left the church.

The Tatum's had to go back to Dalton that night. I was so overjoyed, I wanted to go out and sing Christmas carols. Nobody would go with me not even the kids in the neighborhood.

About 9:00 pm, I went a block away and stood under a street light singing as loud as I could. "Joy to the world, the Lord has come..." When I heard a voice inside someone's home. "Shut up boy, go home or Santa is not going to visit you." I went home, but that did not damper my joy of Christmas that year.

The bad Christmas time, was when I woke to see some fantastic toys under the tree. I started to play with them when Dad came into the living room and said," those are not for you, they are for your brother." Those toys were for much older kids and not for infants, there was even an electric train set.

Mom told dad she never wanted my brother to have that train set because it was electric and could electrocute my brother. I got it. I guess it would not bother her if I was zapped with a jolt.

Dad told me he will grow up having them later. I was pointed the corner of the room. There was a 22 rifle with a scope. (By the way the next Christmas I received a 16-gauge shotgun) It would be a few years before I would benefit from these guns.

I found out later, listening to mom talking to a neighbor, that the guns were gifts from the City of Cartersville. (Dad was the city manager at that time) Dad hated guns – he swore he did not want to touch a gun after what he went through in France (WWII). Cartersville being a small rural town in Georgia, everyone went hunting and fishing, everybody had guns and fishing equipment. Dad had only fishing equipment and a small aluminum boat.

The ugly happened that same Christmas, my family went to Calhoun Ga. There mom's entire family was present at my aunt Ruby's house. She and her family had a large chicken farm. The farm had long narrow buildings filled with thousands of chickens. That was off limits to kids like me. Aunt Ruby did not want the chicks to get spooked.

Granny and KawKaw Smith lived right down the road. Their house was small and you had to be very careful. Granny Smith dipped snuff and had her spit cans all over the house. If you knocked one over, you had to clean it up. It was so nasty looking; I would have rather cleaned up a pig pen than those spit cans. KawKaw had much of this blacksmith stuff in a shed. Often my cousin, Gary and I would play in that shed.

KawKaw was what we called our grandfather Smith (mom's dad); his actual name was Emory Smith; his grandfather was a Cherokee scout in a Confederate unit in the American civil war. He was killed and buried in Nashville at the Civil War cemetery.

Back at Aunt Ruby's house, the smell of Southern cooking filled the air with turkey and ham but the best smell was that of good ole sweet tater pie. The house and yard were over flowing with relatives and their kids. It was warm that year for Christmas and many stayed outside until it was time to open presents.

Because there were so many kids (cousins and siblings), it had been arranged that all the cousins had drawn names so that each one would have a present. One by one the names were called until the last present was taken. Even my toddler brother got a gift that year.

After searching and finding nothing under the tree for me, my favorite uncle came to console me while I was crying on the back porch. He told me that he found my gift and pulled out of his wallet a five-dollar bill.

"Don't tell anybody, this is our secret." He said with tears in his eyes. That was big money back in those days. It was spent it back in Cartersville without my parents knowing that I had it. I used it to go to the movies on Saturday in downtown Cartersville.

I did not know that there would be many more holidays that would ignite an unanswered question... *is there something wrong with me?* The anger would begin to develop in me when I was in the sixth grade far away from Cartersville.

From that time on I felt there was some kind of reason for the feelings of being rejected both from mom and dad's sides of the family. There would be times whiles visiting the families, nobody would speak a word to me, not even a greeting however my sister and brother were flooded with attention.

On dad's side most of the time I was all alone unless the Segar family came. - dad's sister My aunt's three boys and I would play around the house and many times get ourselves into mischief getting and scolding's. I don't remember who said it but one time I heard a grown-up say, "Stay away from him, he is nothing but trouble." (Meaning me)

There were only two overwhelming reasons that brought great joy at that home, Papaw's devil's food cake with a thick creamy frosting. The other reason was even better, his homemade banana pudding that was so rich, it would make a king cry with delight.

My sister, and my younger brother would not have to go to dad's parent's home. It seemed very unfair that they got to stay in that big wonderful house of the Tatum's that I loved so much. But I had no say I had to go even if I did not want to.

I had only one from Dad's side (Aunt Frankie) and only two from mom's side (Aunt Maude and Uncle J. L.) that seemed to accept me. Aunt Frankie could not have children. Anytime around her, I would be smothered with hugs of love. One time I visited her when I was in the Army and she gave me a hundred-dollar bill. (a month's pay for a private).

I began to feel very negative feelings from the majority of both mom and dad's families. It was very rare that anyone would even speak to me. For a long time, well into my teens, I kept wondering why I felt like an outsider while around both families.

There were good memories of Christmas times in Cartersville were when dad took me up to Redtop Mountain to cut down a Christmas tree. A fresh cut tree had always filled the house with a rich pine scent. We would cut a tree, close to Lake Allatoona where I would learn to swim in summer, one year.

I don't ever remember us ever having an artificial tree. It would be well into my adulthood before I would experience a true heartwarming Christmas. That would come when I had a real relationship with Christ.

When dad became city manager of Cartersville, evenings before Christmas, as a family, we would fill bags with fruits, nuts, and candies for the employees of the City of Cartersville. I think that was the only time the family was working together, which made Christmas richer those years.

Moving up to the Christmas of 1966 looking for memories

This would become the saddest holiday I would ever experience. The wonderful Christmases of the past would no longer happen because of the radical changes made by progress. This Christmas was the last I would ever spend in Georgia. It still breaks my heart, but knowing that I have those wonderful memories of past Christmas times.

I was twenty at the time. I had some vacation built up a work, needed a break. I had a very negative on-going situation with my girlfriend and needed to get away.

The family was planning to spend Christmas once more in Dalton Ga. I decided that I would go early to spend about three weeks and then ride back with the folks. I didn't mind hitch hiking and from Melbourne, I got rides all the way to Atlanta. In Atlanta the couple I rode with last, dropped me off at the bus station. From there I got a bus to Dalton.

I was glad to take the bus back to Dalton taking old highway 41 the road I was very familiar with. Arriving in Dalton, I walked to my favorite Aunt and uncle's house. They had sold the old home and moved a few houses up the street.

They were no longer living in the massive house they once lived in. I just wanted to see the house one more time. My horror came when I saw the house was not there, they had torn it down to build a commercial type building that officed the Salvation Army. Instantly my heart was aching and yearning to go back in that wonderful place.

I met my cousin Jan at the door of the new home up the street. She had been married and had in infant baby boy, Mark. It was good to be there. The furniture, decor and pictures on the walls from that old large home filled my mind with wonderful memories of past years in my playful, adventurous youth.

I decided to take a long walk towards another place I treasured called Dug Gap. Dad's friend Mr. G. had a large farm-like home there. My family spent just as much time there as we did our relatives. Their place was at the western side of Dalton.

I had just walked over the last ridge to get there when I was horrified. Everything was gone. There was a dirt path wider that a football field. Getting closer I saw the sign they were constructing an intersection for the new Intrastate highway. As I looked down towards Rocky Face. Everything was gone.

I walked through the compacted red dirt heading westward to find another site where they were going to build a Holiday Inn. I thought to myself, *will I ever be able to fine that path to the gap?*

Relief came when I found the narrow path to Dug Gap next to a road under construction over the pass at Dug Gap ridge. That small path led me to places filled with wonder and memories as a young lad.

I managed to find the rock formations I used to play on as a kid. This place not only faced Dalton; you could see all of Dalton as well as seeing the Blueridge mountains to the east and Fort Mountain. The sky was crystal clear that day.

For we Boomers, progress would erase the of joys and contentment of those special places. I am sure that the newer generations would treasure these changes from old to new. The new generations would continue to embrace change as their own.

I don't remember how long I sat there at the gap while memories filled my mind with deep sadness that things were not going to be the same ever again. That would be the last of the *wonder years* we had spent Christmas in Dalton. Future trips would be few and far between. However, no more Christmas times, everything was gone that had sparked those memories.

VACATION - LOSING FRIENDS - A BURNING CROSS - MOVING TO FLORIDA

(Back to the 1950's in Cartersville.)

S ometime in the late 1950s, the family went on vacation to Panama City Florida. Many from Georgia and Alabama consider Panama City beach to be the *choice* vacation destination. It was near and it was cheap and convenient. It had turned out to be a bad experience for the family at that particular time.

The horror of family fights mixed with alcohol killed the joy of a family vacation. What made it worse, dad had one of his coworkers share the vacation house rental with our family. Dad spent all of his time with him and his wife. The future would paint a different scenario for our family in that town. We did not spend much time doing tourist stuff that I remember. It was a despicable what we experienced during that vacation.

That vacation became the pinnacle of negative changes to develop in the next few years.

There were a couple of good vacations we'd as a family that brings some good memories. One vacation, was going to be visiting my sister and her family in Cleveland Ohio. My younger brother, still an infant at that time, stayed in Dalton with the Tatum's, while mom, dad, my sister, myself and cousin Jan did a road trip up north.

That was a fantastic good time. From Georgia through Tennessee, Kentucky and on to Ohio where my other sister Ginny and her family lived. Cleveland was nice, but Lake Erie stunk! It seemed the lake was where everybody threw their trash.

From there we traveled to New York State, to see Niagara Falls, then on to New York city. I remember a giant bill board in times square of a man smoking a cigarette. The sign actually blew out smoke rings. It reminded me of painter Joe.

On down to Philadelphia to see the sites there; then on to Washington D.C. In those days you could and we did take a tour of the White House. Finally, down through the Blueridge mountains and back home in Georgia.

Another good vacation is when we went to the Great Smoky Mountains and camped. That experience years later would edge me to walking a part of the Appalachian Trail. Dad rented a camper he could pull with the car. The first night, I slept in a large opened tent. After that night I slept in the car because a small bear came into the tent and licked my feet. (That was enough of that)

CHANGE IS COMING -LEAVING HOME AND HERATIGE

The summer of 1956, I found out that two of my very close friends were moving. My best friend, Lewis was across town and attending a different school. It was very lonely in the neighborhood. I would walk long distances to be with friends that lived across town, especially Lewis.

With my good friends not in the neighborhood There were two neighborhood girls that I experienced very strange events with. I had turned ten when one of the younger girls came to visit me.

We went down to a creek close to the house. She wanted to show me something that her dad had been reading and wanted to asked me what I thought. In a paper bag she pulled out a new issue of a man's' magazine called Playboy.

She thumbed through the photos, mostly topless ladies. I am thinking, *Here we go again just like that time with Billy on Maybelle Street.* Being much older and very curious, I continued to look at the photos with her. I told her she had better take it back or we both would be in trouble. I did not understand why she would show this stuff to me. Was she worried about her dad or just wanted to get me attention?

Several weeks later another girl who was about fourteen years would old often would babysit my baby brother. One evening she babysat my younger brother when my folks and my sister went out. They did not trust me to watch my brother. Cloth diapers back then were a struggle to change for a young boy.

I would just watch television. At ten I was on the tall size for a boy my age. Sometimes I would talk to the sitter – small talk stuff until one day she said something I did not understand at first.

"Hey Rick, I have an idea, if you let me see you, I will let you see me."

I responded, "What is there to see?" At that moment she started to unbutton her shirt exposing two half lemon sized breast with nipples so small you could not see them.

Well, being very simple minded, I unbuttoned my shirt and showed her mine. She got angry and that was it. That thing that happened with Billy on Maybelle Street stuck with me a long time. I knew she want to experiment with me and I was having not part of it.

One night in the late summer that year while having a sleep over with a couple of friends from school, in our back yard, I awoke with the sound of grown men talking in our front yard. A few moments later, I saw a distinct reflection of a fire off the trees in our yard. Panicked, I grabbed a garden hose to put out the fire.

I was frozen with fear when I saw the image of a cross burning in our front yard. "Start hiring more white people are there will be trouble" I heard one of the men speak.

I was lied to later saying the Klan had the wrong yard and they were not really Klan members because they were not in their robes. In a small town, everybody knows everybody. Dad was the city manager and he had the power to hire or fire anyone he wanted. All in town knew where we lived. Even at my age, I knew it was for dad.

A couple of months passed when that winter, dad landed a job as the new city manager of Panama City Florida. Right after the New Year I left my good friends, school mates, and that wonderful house we lived in. To this day, I believe that

Dad had to leave because of the cross-burning incident in our yard. No one will convince me that it was not. I experienced it, nobody else did.

The day came in January for us to leave. As the moving truck left, mom, myself, my baby brother and our dog slowly drove away from our home. That was the best home we ever lived in it was the center of neighborhood activities, especially with the kids.

I cried when all of my 6th grade class stood out of the school to bid their farewells holding up homemade signs. My sister had the privilege to stay back with friends in order to finish school that year. That really began to burn inside me. I was 10tenand she was fifteen.

Dad had left a few days early to get things ready for us. For me there was the excitement and mystery of this upcoming life. Panama City would usher me into puberty and then into my teens. Things were going to be very different and I would have to make some radical changes.

Arriving in Panama City Florida, it seemed to be a whole different world. We stayed in a motel close to downtown while we waited for the moving van to unload our furniture where we were supposed to live.

This vacation town was going to be my home. The lifestyle would be making big adjustments from the small towns in the foothills of the Appalachian Mountains, to a large city that catered to tourist and a smelly papermill along with two military bases.

Now my world would be sand, magnolia trees, bayous, and Spanish moss hanging from oak trees mixed with the putrid smell of a paper mill across the bayou and the stench and horrible taste of sulfur in the water mixed with all kinds of new insects and reptiles.

Panama City was spread out several miles long and wide. You could have put several Cartersville towns within the city limits. Each area within the town had their own distinct names. We lived in the "Cove" area on the far eastern side of the town.

Dad had been hired due to his experience with construction and contracting. In the years to come there be major projects the city would develop. There were going to build two new marinas, one marina included a new auditorium, city hall office building and a library. The next few years, Panama City took on a new look. In time the city became the main attraction in the Florida panhandle.

FLORIDA AND THE ROUGH CHANGES

You would think that Florida would be vacation paradise year-round, but in the panhandle, it can get wet and cold in the Fall and Winter. That first January it snowed, even though it did not stick. Sometimes there would be ice sheets on the shallow parts of the bayou.

Upon our arrival, dad had surprised us, he had already bought a home on that far Eastern part of the town. He also had another big surprise for us. Our next-door neighbors would be the Nealy's, the family that had lived across the street when we first moved to Cartersville, Ann Nealy was mom's best friend.

I believe Dad did that to make mom happy. Immediately the Nealy's would introduce us to all the neighbors. It made us comfortable. Most of the kids in the neighborhood were close to my age while a couple were my sister's age.

Even though the house seemed to be smaller than the home in Cartersville, it had four bedrooms rather that the three we had before.

First of all, the tap water was horrible – sulfur taste and smell. Dad had a special filter installed to make it a little better and it did get rid of the smell, but that did not kill the taste. Cokes would be my stationary drink.

Almost as soon as we got there, I had to enroll in school. Cherry Street Elementary was seven short blocks from our new home. I never had the thought that I would be a laughing stock on my first day.

I wore my old jean overalls, a white tee shirt and high-top sneakers and a denim jacket. It was the common wear back in Cartersville for boys my age in the country.

Things were very different in Florida and in their schools. I would find out the hard way.

That first day I went in to the classroom, it was mid-January. When I walked in the whole class started laughing at me. I heard one kid say, "Look out the hillbillys are here." I noticed that all of them were wearing preppy kind of clothes, what we might wear back in Carterville for church or wedding. Those kids were stylist to say the least.

I begged mom to get me some new clothes. Even though the laughter stopped it was a few weeks before I began to look like I belonged. Actually, by that time I had made many friends, I guess it was a novelty to have someone new that wasn't from Florida.

Some of those friends I made, would last well through high school and would become very close.

LOOKING BACK – THE EVENT THAT STARTED

MY REBELLIOUS ATTITUDE IN FLORIDA

 As I look back at an event where the worst of my attitude developed, I have to go back to a 6th grade experience in 1957. This was going to be the catalyst that launched my rebellious spirit.

At the end of the first school year, the custom of Cherry St. Elementary school was that the 6th graders would put on a show (musical). We were grouped into different groups to perform. My group was to sing the Mickey Mouse song and we all had the mouse ears and white gloves.

We had practiced for months. Mom and dad were well informed of the event that would start at 7:00 pm that Friday evening. Dad's secretary's son was in the same Mickey Mouse group. Surely, they would not miss that.

They dropped me off at the school and said they would be right back. The school cafeteria also served as an auditorium. My group's performance was the next to last event. As my group went out to perform, I looked for my parents but they were not there.

The program was over at 9:00 pm and my parents were not there. I waited about 30 minutes until the school janitor told me I should walk home. I did walk home, fuming all the way. When I got home, my parents had just pulled up in the driveway. Nothing was said.

The next day I heard that my parents had gone to another school across town to see a city councilman's son perform in his school. Things like this would continue to happen for the next few years. Why am I being treated this way...answer was coming soon after I would get my driver's license? I was treated much better back in Cartersville.

That summer I spent the majority of time with a boy across the street that had a concussion from a bad fall. He spent the most of the summer bedridden. His parents were grateful that I had spent time with him almost every day watching television and playing games. We got real silly watching Captain Kangaroo imitating him and mister Green Jeans.

LIFE ON THE WATER

Watson Bayou was just across the street from our house. Some of the neighbors gave us permission to use their docks for fishing, boating and swimming. I took them up on it, the fishing was great, with a shrimp net you did not have to buy bait. Swimming was a daily routine from early spring to mid-fall whereas fishing was all year round. Learning to water ski only added to the joy of living life on the water.

Almost everyone had boats in that part of the city. The waters, bayous and bays there were like highways and roads to get around.

The beaches were covered by a fine white sand that looked like snow. Walking on it made a barking sound. The water at the beach was a light green color next to the shore that turned into a deep aqua blue a few yards off shore. It was a fine place to fish if you had the right bait and equipment.

During those years, there were not many hotels and motels along the beach. Along the beach strip there were homes and beach homes for vacation rentals. There were several amusement establishments that locals and tourist could enjoy. Today if you were to drive through the Panama City beaches, it would be difficult to see the beach and water due to all the buildup.

The first summer, dad bought a sixteen-foot boat with a 35HP motor. Fishing and trolling as well as water skiing, that was going to be great fun that the boat would provide for the family.

I heard him talking to mom that he was going to name the boat after my brother. My sister got to finish her school year in Cartersville and now, the boat name! Even I knew boats were supposed to be named after girls or a fishing term. He could have named it the Clara Lee, after mom. Things were rapidly changing within the home environment. In Cartersville it was not that bad but now in Florida things were changing very fast. Panama City and Bay County were not dry. You could buy alcohol anywhere. That soon, would become a major problem.

I don't hate my brother and sister, I love them more that they know, the problem was never with them it was how my parents treated them in comparison to how they treated me.

For years, I would keep asking myself, *"What is wrong with me that I am treated the way my parents treated me. Especially after moving to Florida?* Things were fine back in Georgia until we moved. Florida would create a whole new scenario.

It was more from dad than mom. At times he was downright mean to me. Saying awful things – "your skull is so thick an Xray they could not find your brain."

Mom was not as bad but would take credit for anything I did right, comparing me to my wonderful sister and brother and others when I did things wrong... *Why can't you be like your sister – ever worse why can't you be more like so and so's son.* I would think to myself, *why can't I just be me.* I was never good enough for the standards my parents set for me. Yet, I perceived that my sister and brother seemed to meet their expectations.

Once again, the feelings of rejection married with anger began to burn inside of me. Many days ahead that anger would burst forth into negative rageful behavior in various forms of vandalism, being a bully to others, and in trouble with the local law.

I won't say where, but one late evening with a few of my rowdy pre-teen friends, we filled a small metal tube with gun powder we obtained by emptying shot gun shells. We did not realize how powerful it was going to be.

We put it in a door jamb one night of a certain old school building and lit the fuse, ran a few yards away when suddenly a thunderous blast completely blew the door to bits scattering bits of wood all over everything including us. It was scary and yet thrilling.

It was even empowering to a young boy in his pre-teens when parents had suddenly become so negative in this new environment. The other boys also had troubles in their home life. A couple of them, their parents had divorced.

It would get to the point that I would lose control. I became a bully picking on the weakness of others. I wanted to hurt somebody because I was hurting. I was always in trouble with the law especially late at night when kids my age were supposed to be at home.

The city police department had programs for troubled kids. I think they knew I was a part of the door explosion.

With no choice, I was linked up with the group. The group was involved with several community projects. Once a month we went to the gun range as a part of the Junior NRA program. It was nice to have adults pay attention to kids like me. But it did not change my feelings about life at home, but it was an outlet needed to control negative behaviors.

Boating and life on the water was an escape for me. There were many times I wanted to get as far away as I could from home. It was good that I had families and friends that not only let me go boating with them, but taught me how to handle and drive their boats.

My parents never knew them, they were families of my classmates that lived on the waterfront in the Cove area of town.

One day a miracle happened, dad actually began to allowed me to drive his boat but only when the family was in it and when dad fished (trolling for fish in the gulf.) Seeing how I handled the boat, he let me drive it, but only if he was in it.

A year or so after. I drove the boat on my own, mostly to gas it up and prep it for fishing in the Gulf of Mexico. He told me numerous times "You're not ready to take the boat out on your own yet, I was always taking other people's boats out especially a family across the street, I even taught them how to handle their boat after they had bought one.

One day some visitors came down from Cartersville. They had a nephew my age. The boy Al was my age Al wanted to take the boat for a spin all by himself. Dad let him. I stayed on the dock. After a while, he came back to the dock. I yelled, "You're going way too fast." Too late, he hit the dock making a large hole in the plywood/wood framed boat.

I had stayed on the dock while Al took the boat out. (Guess who got the blame even though I stayed on the dock).

I did not say anything. After over a years' experience I was not allowed to take the boat on my own and yet Al, my age who had never driven a boat in his life, wrecked it on his first try. It was easy for dad to say yes to others but not towards me. Tension and hurt were building up within me.

I kept asking myself over and over, *What is wrong with me, am I adopted?* I did recognize that dad like to play the big shot when we had visitors, after all he was the manager of the main tourist destination for those from Alabama and Georgia.

From then on, I borrowed boats and went fishing, shrimping, and going for scallops at times making a little money for a fifteen-year-old boy, and yes, I did bring some home thinking I would get a pat on the back, but that never came. I stopped bringing my catch home.

There were long periods of time I did not speak to mom or dad. If they asked a question, I would either nod a yes or no or shrug my shoulders. I felt like, I wanted them to feel what I was feeling.

THE STRAW THAT BROKE THE CAMMEL'S BACK

One day, dad had promised that just he and I would go fishing in the gulf. King mackerel were running and so were the ling-cod. The day before, I gassed up the boat, bought bait, got the fishing rigs ready and filled up the cooler with ice to put the fish we caught in.

Early that Saturday morning I was ready at the dock, when I heard some voices coming down. It was dad and a couple of friends visiting from Cartersville. I didn't think much about it. All were in the boat when I jumped on the bough after releasing the boat from the dock when I heard dad's voice, "Where do you think you are going." Not speaking a word, I jumped back on the dock, never to get in that boat again. From that day, I would avoid any conversation with my family...

To my shame looking back, I hated them and would not even call on them using the words mom and dad. I would just speak what I wanted or made comments. Hatred for them was beginning to grow.

It was not long after that dad took me to a professional counselor. At the same time, dad was also seeing a counselor as well. It seemed that the counselor that dad had, gave him some good advice but dad did not follow it in the manner pre-scribed. He told my dad to do a father – son activity that would help us to bond.

My counselor wanted me to talk about my feelings. I bot-tled up, thinking as a young teen. How is that going to change things. After that we talked about sports, school and other things, that did not matter that much.

Here is what happened after the counseling, since I wanted to use our boat by myself. Dad and I were going to build a boat.

Dad got plans to build a tiny boat six feet by three feet at the widest. The plans were actually for a sail boat. Of course, I had no say in what kind of boat I wanted.

He was supposed guide me building the boat myself. Rather than that, he did all the work himself, including painting the boat, I was just the gopher – you know – go for this, go for that. He placed a 15HP motor on it that he used in Georgia when we lived there. The motor was not designed for salt water nor was it powerful enough for skiing.

In a very short time, the motor was damaged by the salt water and could not be used, I could only paddle the boat. Yep, while all my friends were driving their boats by themselves, including a young boy I knew that was three years younger than me and my dad's secretary's son that was my age and in the same classes. I had a boat that would sink if you had more than two people in it. Strange that my parents would continually compare me with others my age but not allow me the same privileges as those they compared me with.

A few weeks later the boat disappeared from the dock it was moored to. I was glad, even embarrassed to have it. Some of my friends called it the kiddy boat because it was so small. "Hey Rick, did you steal that from a carnival ride?"

The next advice the counselor gave was that I was supposed to go on an excursion with mom and dad.

By that time, dad had bought a much larger boat that was diesel powered and classified as a day cruiser and had a nice cabin area. It was much larger making it steady even in heavy seas in the Gulf. The small boat named after my brother was sold.

That excursion was even worse, yet. That weekend all my friends were having a big skiing party and camp out. I told my parents, "Let's go another time." The answer was no, of course! I believe if it was my sister, the answer would be "Yes of course!"

Saturday of that week Dad took us in his new boat on a roundtrip 200-mile journey on the Intracoastal Waterway from Panama City to Appalacacola, Florida. It was late Sunday afternoon when we got back.

Very few words were spoken on that trip, Mom and dad slept in the cabin, I slept on the floor of the boat becoming a feast for the massive swarms of mosquitoes. I did not have a blanket or pillow only a cushion. Yep, that was some bonding! Somehow, I would make sure I would never go with them or do anything with them again other than going back to Georgia for vacations or Christmas.

One day, Mom's aunt that passed away. The family was going to drive up to Columbus Georgia. I was supposed to go, but somehow disappeared just as they were about to leave. I knew they were going to be angry and thought they had locked me out of the house.

I had plans to visit and spend the day with one of my friends. My rationale was if my sister could stay back in Cartersville and Dad's boat named after my brother, and a boy my age could drive the boat alone, I could do what I wanted, from that time on, my anger would turn into bitter rebellion and acts of rage. While they were gone, I smoked what was left of dad's cigarettes and had me one of mom's beer.

Inside my being rather than feeling liberated, I felt like I was dying having no hope for change.

When they came back, I got the belt on my back and legs. The marks lasted for a couple of weeks. But I was not bothered by that, it was the norm for me. Over the years I never witnessed my siblings punished with a belt or switch.

Swimming from spring to fall, along with a lot of water skiing, you might say I was becoming a water man. I had passed the junior lifeguard training and a few years later I would be and official lifeguard. At that time, you had to be eighteen to get a job as a lifeguard in the state of Florida.

Water activities and close friends gave me the escape I needed in dealing with the dysfunctional family dynamics that were developing at home, and was growing more troublesome as time passed. I was much closer and more accepted by other families than my own, including the family of my dad's secretary.

A CRUSH – MAKING FRIENDS – A NEW CHURCH

Across the street from my house was a cute gal close to my age, she was a bit older. I learned much from her. I remember the neighborhood kids threw me a birthday party for me. All there were in their early teens, I had just turned thirteen. That was very special because the kids planned it all on their own, my family didn't even know it was happening.

When it got dark one of the kids, suggested we play, "Spin the bottle." At my turn it landed on that cute gal. we went to a dark side of the house that evening. As I stood there a minute or so I said, "Let's go back now that is long enough." "Wait, you have not kissed me yet.' She told me as she leaned into me. My first kiss, right on the lips, I was in the clouds, wow!

Now that she had me hooked, she invited me to go to church with her and her family on Sundays. How could I say no?

My first Sunday at that little Methodist church, the youth class was extraordinary. All had Bibles and if you did not bring one, they gave you one – even to take home and keep. For a short time, my spiritual pilgrimage was moving again.

I really loved and enjoyed the people in the neighborhood. I would spend much more time with them than at my house until something new was added to our home.

Dad had surprised the family with a new television set, it was the first color tv set in the neighborhood. At first there were only two shows that aired in color. On Sunday nights there was Bonanza and on Wednesdays there was the Disney show. Sunday was when our house was packed with people in the neighborhood. To view this new technology. Within a few months almost all had a color TV. By then more color shows were broadcast.

One summer, some of my friends in school said I should go out for little league baseball. I walked to a ball park close to our house for tryouts. I did well, especially for the little experience I had from playing ball on school grounds back in Cartersville. The coaches told me that I needed my own glove in order to be on a team. I told dad and he said he would pick up a glove after work.

I was excited until dad came home without the glove. I missed practice that evening. I reminded dad to get me a glove.

The next day he came home with a glove. What was to be my glove was a cheap plastic replica for little kids. "I can't use that!" with dad's quick reply, "You will use that G... damn glove or shove it, where the sun doesn't shine." *Wow*, all I could say and think of. Why does a grown man talk that way to his son?

That evening he drove me to the park and dropped me off to make sure I went; he had a meeting that night. As I walked into the dugout, the kids and coaches began laughing at me and my plastic glove. I turned around and walked away. As I left the ball park I tossed the glove in a trash can.

Baseball would be over for me for good. One day in the future, I would find that special sport that would be so suited with me, I would participate in it well into my senior years.

When I married and had kids and grandkids, I made double efforts to support them in any endeavor they wanted to participate in.

The rest of the summer I spent with older friends that had boats. Together we would water ski, swim at the Cove Hotel next to the bay. I would only come home to bath, eat and sleep. At home, my parents did not know what I was doing or where I was, and I really did not care. I don't think they did either.

Many times, I sneaked out at night to hang out with the older kids I knew. It was easy to do that. Since my brother slept with my sister in her bed, I had the room all to myself. It was easy to slip out through the screen in the window.

One night I came home and the screen was locked, little did my folks know I had a technique to open it and climb in. Of course, when school was on, it was a place to enjoy attention from staff and friends. I had a strong desire to be at school rather than be at home.

HIGHER GRADE LEVELS

The seventh thru ninth grades were called junior high school, in those days. Most of the friends I had made were all going to the same school. The school was located about six miles west of where we lived therefore most of us rode the city bus to and from school.

My sister took the high school kids and one that went to the same junior high, with the car dad bought, but I had to ride the bus. My sister was getting in on the act with Mom and dad. From that time my affection for her dwindled.

Again, I asked myself the question, "What in the hell is wrong with me and what the hell is wrong with my family; why do I always feel like an outcast in my own family?" Don't get me wrong there were times that things seemed normal, I would say about 25 percent of the time. It was the 75 percent that I felt like an outcast.

Though my grades were not that great, it seemed I got along with my teachers. Unlike many kids, I looked forward to attending classes. Kids who do not get attention at home will get attention elsewhere.

Somehow it had been suggested that I join the Junior Police program. At that time, it was for troubled kids immediately I found it was the same group I was linked up with for troubled kids earlier. We worked the crosswalks at the school and on weekends would go on a camp or work on community projects.

Our supervisor was a retired policeman. Although he was in charge of the program, other officers that were off duty, often would come and help out. Many times, that retired officer would pick me up from home and take me to his house to have dinner with him and his wife. I noticed that they were Christians, not only did they pray at meals, they prayed specifically for me.

The junior police program was mostly doing school crossings and working the parking lots directing traffic during high school events. At the junior high school, it gave us troubled kids some clout.

One day during physical education class someone had tattled on a group of us that we were all telling nasty jokes and using curse words.

When the coach heard about it. all of us wound up in his office. He told us he would send a note home to our parents or give us a task. We all chose the task. He told us," This will be your task to write the Ten Commandments 100 times." The coach had them posted on his office wall.

While writing these commandments, I had a very strong objection to the one about honoring my father and mother. They were great parents to my siblings, but to me... not! I thank God, down through the years this would change one day. That would be many years later.

I did not hate my parents, I just wanted to feel like they loved me and treated me like they treated my siblings on an equal playing field. I would not feel that until well into their retirement years. How could I honor them like the commandment said?

I would try from time to time with the money I made fishing, paper routes and later artwork. I would buy them nice gifts for birthdays and Christmas. Only mom thanked me one time when I had bought her a necklace. It was becoming more difficult to even say that I loved my family, it was rare during my school years I felt any love towards them.

As I wrote, more and more, these commandments for the coach, these commands began to become etched to my mind and my heart. As I look back, I believe that God was speaking to me in a personal way even though I was not yet a true, born-again Christian.

I had developed a respect for that coach. Someone cared enough to point us to God through his word. Now days a teacher like that would get fired.

Taking the bus home from school became good fun for kids our age. We all would get off the bus at a small strip mall close to home and hang out at the drug store, they had the stools at the counter and booths to sit in drinking our cherry cokes and root beer floats and lots of girls. We boys were at that age the girls caught our eyes; Flirting was the name of the game. Many times, we would not go home until dark.

By the ninth grade a drive-in diner opened across from the drug store. It had booths, tables and something the drug store did not have, a jukebox with all the current tunes.

Well into high school I had some great times there with fantastic friends. As I look back, if I did not have those wonderful friends, I know I would have been incarcerated in a boy's reform school north of Panama City. The friends I had knew where to draw the line as not to get ourselves into deep trouble. They were closer than my family.

One of the older good friends had a girlfriend. The whole gang would hang out at her house on weekends when nothing else was going on. Her dad was one of the nicest men I've known. He would come out on the porch and asked us about our lives. Then, much like my grandfather, would talk to us about Jesus. The older boy that we came with, became a Christian. The father of the girl was also a deacon at a local Baptist church. Soon the older boy was keeping us all I line. (Positive influence)

Each summer after school -from Junior - High was spent doing much the same fishing, skiing, and hanging out with friends while I did my best to avoid even going home to clean and change, now I could do that with my older friends' homes while their parents were out.

THE WORLD WAS CHANGING AND BECOMING CONFUSING

In the 1950's it was Elvis, 45 records, original rock and roll, old cars, drag strips, duck tail haircuts for guys and for us hanging out at the diner and many other things that were trending fads.

In the local Auditorium that the city had built there were many popular rock groups that came and performed. The city even had Broadway plays to come. Because dad was the city manager and all the employees at the auditorium knew me, I got in free every time, and I got to go backstage a few times.

One time Fats Domino and other black groups came for a concert. When I got there the staff told me to sit up stairs. I was the only white person there. So, what, the music was great and many of the black people that saw me gave me a thumbs up and a smile.

Dad got excited one time when one of his starlets he knew from living in Hollywood did a play there. We all went back stage to meet her. She acted in a play, "Dark at the top of the stairs".

The 1960's brought boomers into our teens and our world, as it seemed, was spinning out of control. Another war in a place we had never heard of, Vietnam.

All were tired of wars and yet they still came, many boomers would not live to see the end of the 60s or 70s because of the war in Vietnam. Including several of my classmates and friends.

Long silent, fearful weekends came with the Cuban Missile Crisis in October 1962. Everyone thought we were on the brink of World War three. Those of us in Florida were told that Cuba and the Russians would hit Florida first because of the multiple military bases. There were two large bases in the Panama City area.

Families all over were building bomb shelters. At schools we were being drilled to take cover if an atomic bomb hit the city. One time a jet from the local Air Force base, flew over the school breaking the sound barrier, so loud was the sonic boom it wound up breaking windows. We though an atomic bomb had hit, we all scrambled under our desk, some crying others screaming, and those that were silent with fear.

Everybody would stay home most of the time. (Not me, I hated being at home) Many thought this could be the end of mankind with so many countries having atomic bombs. What made things more frightening was the Kennedy assassination, then later his brother Bobby. We all thought the Russians were behind this, asking to ourselves who or what is going to be next?

Each day we boomers would live with the fear of not knowing from day to day what our world was going to look like or even if we were going to have a future.

For a few years then, everyone was glued to the news on television and the radio. News was the lifeline to the facts. Can you believe that news in those days, news was actually reliable?

We had people like Walter Cronkite and David Brinkley. Who would have ever thought we would live to see the day when the media would make up their own stories and interpretation of the news rather than just telling the truth? Years later we were told that the news had to be properly interpreted. (What a bunch of bull)

Soon we needed escapes from reality. Boomers like myself began seeing movies and TV shows that related to us.

Annette and Franky beach movies were my favorite. We had television shows made for us. Bandstand, and Hootenanny was the ones I liked among several other shows. I loved the Beverly Hillbillys, the real McCoy's and the Andy the sheriff of Mayberry reminded me of Georgia.

We also had those things that had been regular for teens for a long time like sporting events and parties, lots of parties. Summer, it was the beach and water activities with more parties. That was our escape. Locally, there were teen clubs at high schools for shooting pool and dancing. That was usually when the weather was bad. The mid-60s brought in a new era, boomers had our own culture, we were more in control of what we wanted rather than what society was Trying to dictate for us to follow. The economics of that time began to cater to our generation because there was a lot of us conceived rightafter the war. We were trendy and active.

Things were changing so fast it was difficult to keep up. We at that age, were seeing what seemed to be our world falling apart, were searching to be a part of something. We needed to feel like we belonged and needed to feel important. For me it there was no comfort at home, only heart ache and frustrations.

By 1965, everybody in American seemed to be protesting something – war, politics even wealth.

Birth control, drugs, sex, R rated movies, porn magazines sold in regular stores. Downright rebellion was becoming symbols of freedom. The adults of that era made us feel like we were abandoned, that was for sure in my home. However, we were considered young adults. The advertising markets zoomed in on us because we had become buyers.

For many it was too much too soon our world was spinning out of control. Many of us boomers would rebel in our own way. Mine would eventually lead to the beach life, day and night. We all wanted to get as far away as possible from life in the main stream.

Many chose to live in communes. Guys went to Canada to avoid being drafted. Many did not want to go to what seemed an endless war that had no logical reason for being.

Some that outright rebelled out west in California they called themselves hippies. The great irony of the Hippie generation is the fact that hippies want to be different and separate themselves from society that for them, was way out of control yet, for some reason they all seemed to look and act the same. Everything was going crazy.

One very positive phase, at that time, was the Jesus movement started up in the later part of the 60's and well into the 70's. Many church groups at that time would develop into major denominations that thrive today. People were searching and many found what they were looking for in Christ. In a couple of years, I had found Christ during that time, but that comes later.

Something else was changing at my home. An elephant started to grow larger in our home. Those who have lived through a dysfunctional, alcoholic home know what the elephant is.

Those that know the elephant have lived through tough painful experiences that were extremely embarrassing when others outside the family noticed it. People that have mental issues blended with alcoholism have a difficult time facing the realities and severe issues within themselves that too often spilled over into family dynamics.

What made things worse was the fact everybody knew what was going on in our home. I would hear from mom's friends and neighbors, "Rick why don't you stay home and take care of your mother?" I would respond, I will give mom the same time and attention as my brother, sister, and dad give her." My brother to young and dad and sis too busy with their lives, with the way I had been treated... NOT GOING TO HAPPEN! I was not about to be the caretaker when others in the family did their own thing, I am just a teen I am going to do my thing.

As the years moved on the problem got worse and more difficult to handle. The memories do not vanish, they will either shape you into similar patterns or force you to rise above to where those things no longer affect you.

It came to the point the elephant wound up multiple times in mental and rehab hospitals, sometimes six months out of the year. Three times after I got my driver license, I was the one who had to pick her up and drive her home. I was the one to search the house for hidden bottles of liquor. I was the one to make sure her medications were for her and not some other name on the bottle she managed to borrow with the excuse that she just wanted to try to see if it worked for her.

Enduring the pain would be a long journey for me that would take me far into my adulthood before I could rise above it with the help of God on my spiritual pilgrimage as well as the education from seminary and my favorite professors, especially John D. Doctor of Psychology. He taught me the dynamics of the disease of alcoholism and mental illness and the effects it has on families. He also had a time share in Hawaii spending quality time helping me to understand the dynamics of a dysfunctional home and how I could overcome the pain and frustrations. Personal counseling from an all-time great professor.

DRIVING - GIRLFRIEND - TRUTH BE KNOWN

Junior high school over, many may age were a bit apprehensive about the next step going to High school. I had some good advice from Mr. Nealy next door, to take two important courses, even if you don't like them. The first course was to take drivers education. The second course recommended was to take typing; not just one semester but a semester each year in high school. I did! In years to come that would prove to be extremely beneficial especially during my stay in the Army.

I continued my art courses in high school meeting some new fantastic friends; one would be a partner in doing art work throughout the town.

The driver's education class was informative and yet the movies they showed of accidents were as gross as horror movies. One movie displayed a highway patrolman using a garden rake to sweep up the remainder of a child that had been mangled in a severe car accident. I thought I was going to puke. I didn't, but others did.

Dad was interested in me driving because he did not want Mom to drive in her condition. There was also the fact that since I passed driver's education with flying colors, his insurance rates were going to drop. I loved driving that 1956 Buick. For some reason dad always had Buicks up until the time he was placed in a care home.

Little did dad know that I had already been driving some of my older friends' cars for over a year' even on the local drag strip. That was actually good experience for me. Even though I did not have a license.

It was not long after getting my driver's license that I met a young girl. We hung out a while with friends and before too long we were going steady. She was my first love, I thought one day when we were older, I would marry her.

One evening we did not have anything to do, when my girlfriend asked to take her to where her parents were at their friend's house. When we went in, they were getting ready to play charades. I could not fathom that these adults wanted us teens to join in. That night, I felt a warmth that I had only felt when I went to Dalton. I was actually treated as an adult even though I was only 17.

In all honesty, I loved her family more than her, it was stable and I felt welcomed. They lived just a few blocks from where I was living. Things were great being with them in their home. So many times, I wished it would be like that at my home.

My grandfather Watkins would come down and visit from time to time. I was bothered, due to the fact that his attention was all to my little brother and none to myself. He always had some gift for my brother, but never me. Mom told me that sometimes he would give my brother a fifty-dollar bill (that was a lot of money in the 60's) and my brother was only nine.

Dad had me to drive him around where ever he wanted to go. Most of the time he wanted to go fishing or attend a Nazarene church. I did not mind him always talking about Jesus and the need to get involved back in church. I liked going to church, if I had people I could relate to.

My problem with my grandfather, I had never received any gift at all. Which made me wonder, why.

One day, happened to be early summer, I wanted to be with my girlfriend that day, but dad wanted me to take my grandfather fishing. I thought this might me an opportunity to get some answers that had been bothering me since I could remember. I was seventeen at that time.

I knew he was and open and honest man and perhaps he could help me to understand some things, after all I am old enough to drive.

In a freshwater lake north of Panama City he rented a small boat and motor, loaded up his fishing equipment and we headed out to a nice quiet shady spot. As soon as we settled in the spot, he opened the usual conversation about me needing Jesus and being involved in a church.

I said that I would listen to anything he had to say if he would give me some honest answers that had been troubling me about both sides of the family and why they seemed to ostracized me.

Then, what he told me not only shocked me but actually made some sense. Finally, I had some answers and years later the information was confirmed by others in the families, as well as my dad right before he died.

Papaw Watkins began to tell me that when I had been born, that I had that platinum blond hair. No one by blood in either mom or dad's side of the family had blond hair like that and that may have made the families suspicious, especially when mom's first husband was supposed to have had blond hair and mom had dated a man in high school that had hair like that; he lived close by to where mom lived.

Many had made jokes about it, but it sure did not help me. If they made jokes, why did they stay away from me when I was with the family?

The story goes on, that when dad had come home from France after the war, that he had to stay on a base in Virginia to complete his military duty because he enlisted late in the later part of the war.

One weekend he had a three-day pass and took a train to Dalton. (His home) for New Year's Eve. He did not have time to visit anyone else and stayed a few hours with mom. Trains in those days were slow because they would stop in every town. He had to get back to Virginia as soon as possible or be AWOL.

I was conceived and born nine months later, September 7, 1946 with that blond hair. Furthermore, neither side of the family knew that dad had come home only a few hours.

Papaw continued to tell me that when he finally came home from the Army, mom was already showing and people were gossiping. Papaw also told me dad was going to go into partnership with a friend in a carpet factory. He had to sell his share to pay for the doctor bill, when I was born. Only rich people could afford health insurance in those days.

Later, dad resented the fact that he had lost out on a very lucrative business that later had grown and was successful. Papaw told me he was angry, extremely angry about that for many years even though he was doing great as a civil servant. I had become the reason he lost out; therefore, I had become his personal scapegoat, the object of his anger. Dad, for the first few years had questioned if I was his or not.

Papaw also told me for years people outside the family would gossip about that, thinking that I was not my dad's child. I was told on mom's side it was all a joke, if it was, why was I treated like an outcast by most of them?

Hearing that I thought, *Why in the world would I become the object of dad's anger and ostracized by family on both sides?* I would write that off as pure country hick ignorance.

After telling me this I asked, "Well, what do you think, do you think that I am dad's son?"

He smiled telling me, "Now, you look just like your dad when he was your age at 17."

My hair was dark at that time the blond hair had altogether disappeared.) Years later, I had seen photos of dad at my age and you could not tell us apart. By then most of the damage had been done to any positive relationships with the families except for a quaint few.

We went back to the car with no fish that day, but to me I had a much better understanding. The understanding still did not excuse the way that my parents and family members treated me in comparison to my siblings. Nor was it an excuse for the majority of the families to have treated me the way they did. To this day I believe most of them actually saw me as being the bastard son of the family.

I am thankful, that day I received much needed answers. But my attitude towards family had grown biter.

By the time I was in my 20's most of the family knew that I was dads without any doubt. That was a big load off my chest even though things did not change for me at home. However, there were some on both sides that had their doubts until I started getting gray hair. By then, some said looked much like dad and even Papaw Watkins.

Years later, before dad went home to be with Jesus, he confirmed that story. I had flown in from Hawaii to attend a conference. Dad wanted me to meet him in Nashville and we would drive down to Louisiana to visit my sister. I feel that he wanted to mend the negative sides of our relationship.

That time together was the first time we had ever a real father to son talk. I will treasure that; it was man to man and not from dad to a wild son. For three days it was dad and myself driving and chatting for hundreds of miles.

Much of what was told to me by his dad was confirmed. His health was fading and he wanted me to see mother. She was already in a care home facility.

He told me of his life, getting married at 15 to a girl 14 and going through a bitter divorce and even kidnapping his daughter. He shared about working as a contractor for the government building military bases in Colorado, and California. While working in Los Angeles, he had an apartment in Hollywood. I got embarrassed when he began talking about his sex life with in Hollywood, while living there.

While living in Hollywood, he would visit the various places and even sign autographs for people thinking he was a star. Later telling of how he got into the army. He had many interesting stories of things that happened during WWII. Because of the nature of the stories, I will not mention them in this book, just remember any war is horrible what people do to their human brothers.

The next time I would see dad was when he was placed in a care home. He had called me to come and help. I flew in from Hawaii at that time and stayed there in his house on Pine Street for a month paying bills that had not been paid in a while.

I tried to get him to sign his checks but his hands were so withered from arthritis, he told me to us his bank card and get cash to pay the bills. I told him I would get the receipts. He had plenty of unpaid bills. I got chewed out by a relative thinking I had spent the money on myself. I only took out money for my airfare to Florida from Hawaii and to put fuel in his car that I was driving. I had my own money and cards, yet he insisted I use his cards.

That month would be the last time I would see him in this world. He would pass 2003. My brother, Terry and Margret Clark were there with him at his bedside.

Art Talent, yours or Mine

One summer, back in the early 1960's, while we were living in Panama City, Florida, my sister was going to a local community college, I was informed there were classes for Junior and High school students. I was encouraged to check it out.

The art class seemed to be interesting, so I signed up commuting with my sister who had classes the same time. I had fun working on some sketches. The teacher wanted us to do a painting of a famous person. I decided to do Shakespeare. The teacher expressed that I had a talent in the creative arts. He loved my Shakespeare (it was a Cartoon rendition that I had based most of my characters after)

Upon hearing that, mother was overjoyed telling me the city was having a local art contest. Artist were to do paintings that depicted scenes in the area.

She bought me an oil painting set. I went across the street and sketched a tug boat docked next to some oil tanks on the bayou. I painted the sketch with the oil paints mom bought.

When entering the contest, I named the painting as "Tug on Watson Bayou." There was no age bracket in the contest, it was sponsored by the chamber of commerce. I won first prize, mainly because the other works turned in did not display local features of the Panama City area. A week later, I was on a local television show along with other artists. (I still have that painting)

Art was a great escape for me. I even did some sculptures and won more awards and prizes with them at the county fairs. Though the years I continued this skill bringing relaxation and satisfaction within me.

My mother paid for me to take some private lessons in art. At last, I was getting some recognition and attention at home for a short while, until a little problem came along. Mom was there to take all the credit.

There was a local newspaper reporter who wanted to interview me, she did not because mom kept interrupting saying how she pushed me to do it and if it had not been for her personally discovering my talent, I would have never found it and would have wound up as a nobody because my school grades were not that great. I am glad the reporter did not report that! A couple of years later in high school that same newspaper was publishing some of my cartoons.

I did continue to pursue art in high school and later in college. As I write this, I still enjoy art. Back then, I even wanted to make it a career one day; but God had other plans for me.

Jeremiah 29:11(NIV) says, "For I know the plans I have for you," declares the LORD, "plans to prosper you and not to harm you, plans to give you hope and a future."

I loved the classes I took both in High school and in Community college. Quickly, finding that it was a great money maker. During high school I had cartoons published in the local newspapers and made signs and displays for stores.

Christmas was the biggest money maker by painting signs and décor in stores and business windows. That was also the most difficult to do because you had to use tempura paint on store windows and paint everything backwards on store front windows. Later I would be painting roadside billboards in the Melbourne Florida area with my good friend, Leon. Art was a great side income for years even while I served in the military.

Looking back, I was very blessed because from the age of 13 to adulthood, I was blessed with continuous jobs and income. Not one penny came from dad or anyone else in the family. Ironically that most of the jobs I was doing while still in school, my parents were not aware of. I guess I had come to the point where I figured – *What's the point?* They wouldn't be interested anyway except for mom trying to rob me of the credit.

I still enjoy working art projects. Later in life I even took up ceramics and woodburning work and model building. One of my wood- burning works somehow, someway wound up on a table seen on the 700 club on a television set.

A WEDDING - HERE WE GO AGAIN – IT'S UNFAIR – STARTING ALL OVER= (1963)

Life in Panama City was coming to a close at the end of 1963.

My sister had been dating a while with a nice guy, I liked him a lot. He took me hunting and fishing a couple of times. It was late that year they were married. The ceremony was one of the largest I had ever experienced. It was the social event of the year in that church.

After the wedding, mom had sent me to get something for her out of the car. Several of the church doors were already locked. By the time I got back the family photos had already been taken, I remember that I was only in one photo. That seemed to be the norm for me with the family.

I don't remember much of the details but dad was on the brink of being let go from his job with Panama City. I do know that politics had a great deal to do with it. I know from elections in the past with ads on TV and the newspaper, politics in the panhandle of Florida were downright cut throat nasty.

In a short period of time right after my sister's wedding. Dad landed a job in central Florida:

That was four hundred miles from Panama City, my girlfriend, my best buddies, and worse of all I was in the middle of my senior year in high school, in anticipation to walk the line with my friends at graduation. These special friends I had for the past six years, to me were closer than my own family, friends that kept me from getting into deep trouble with the law.

The big argument where I blew up in dad's face!

I had friends all over that offered to let me stay with them including the Nealy family that lived next door even my dad's former secretary. "No Rick you will have to go and that is the final answer.

"But Sis got to stay back and she was not even a senior, that is so unfair why don't you lock me up and throw away the key, that is what you are doing to me. Sis is not even you blood, but I am." He did not speak after I said that. I was surprised he did not respond to that statement I made but I remember that was the reddest face on a man that I had ever seen. He was about to raise his hand towards me, but hesitated. (I think he knew that I would have fought back, I was so angry and old enough to take him on.)

Once again, I was on the verge of a major blow-up anger was a regular response to the way I had been treated. Vengeance will be mine was my inner moto. My mind filled with ways and actions that I planned to get back at all of them. Again, I wondered if I really was my dad's son. Maybe Papaw Watkins had made up that story to make me feel better about myself.

Mom was already into deep stages of alcoholism cupped with severe mental illness that would only get worse in our new environment with mom having longer stays ahead in rehab facilities and hospitals.

It was a long drive down to the Melbourne area. There were no intrastate highways although they had begun to do some construction in Florida at that time. I drove the car while mom, my brother and dog sat in the back. All alone in the front? Driving with mom was slow about every half hour, she had to pee or get herself a beer somewhere. If I did not stop for a beer, she would get out of the car with threats not to get back in If I would not let her go in to buy a beer.

Dad had given me instructions to meet him at a motel just north of the town. He came down much earlier to get settled into his new job. Because we had left our old house late, it was about nine in the evening when we arrived. The people that owned the motel were nice enough to let our dog stay in the room.

The next day, dad drove us all around the new town, actually there were two towns next to each other - Melbourne and north of Melbourne, Eau Gallie. Both were very tiny towns exactly next to each other. Little did we know that in years to come this area would become a major metropolitan area in Florida.

We were much closer to the beach than in Panama City. A day coming soon, this beach area would become the center of my activities. In Panama City it was a 16-mile drive to the beach one way. In the Eau Gallie area, it was less than 3 miles to the beach and the Atlantic Ocean.

Finally, dad said, "I have something to show you that I have been looking at. We drove up to a large yellow house with a head high fence on the Western side and a chain-link fence around the backyard.

As we drove in the driveway to the carport, dad told us that a real estate person gave him the keys so we could look it over. It was big, four bedrooms and three bathes. I saw the four bedrooms and two bathrooms I said, "where is the third bathroom?" Dad said as he opened the curtains, "Here it is next to the swimming pool.

All of us were shocked as he told us. "By the way we are not just looking at this house, I have already bought it!"

It seemed as though the pains of leaving friends and a sister behind had begun to heal a little with the anticipation of a private pool. Dad told us that the area was growing due to the operation of the Airforce base and Cape Canaveral (later renamed Kennedy Space Center) There were also several large technical companies in the area.

Nobody wanted to buy the house because there had been people murdered there a few years prior and it was a great bargain to get. (People do get spooked, but how can a dead person harm you?)

This new life, I hoped would change the family dynamics; maybe life would be better and mom would get better. It did not, with mom her condition got worse being further away and not knowing anyone. Again, there were to be longer stays in rehab, leaving myself, dad, and brother alone.

I did not know that the pool was going to be a burden for me. Dad had me clean it all the time and once every year, I would have to paint it with epoxy type paint that was difficult to get off your body, and it was never coming off your clothes.

One time while getting the pool ready to paint by scaping the old stuff off, I fell and hyper extended my left leg. Four months I had to wear a cast. Dad got upset with me because his insurance refused to pay for it. It was my fault I was told that he thought I did it on purpose to get out of the work. (Hey I did put the cast on my leg... who took me to the doctor?)

One of the most thrilling and enjoyable times in the area, was the launching of various rockets from the Space center. Night or day the rocket thrust was so bright it was like a minia-ture sun in the sky. Some of the larger rockets, if you watched them around Cocoa or Titusville, it would feel like a small earthquake when they launched.

The school was about to start up the spring semester. My school records had been sent to a new high school that had just been built to accommodate the growth in the community. School had just started, the next day I was in the administra-tion office checking in. At that time each county in Florida had its own requirements for graduation.

The counselor told me after this semester I could graduate by taking a summer course. I asked if it would be possible to take on a full year. "Why would you do that? You could already be in college by that time."

I told her that I had lost a wonderful senior year with great friends and that I longed for that once-in-a-lifetime experience.

She smiled and acknowledged a deep understanding of how I felt. Looking at my records and knowing that I would need only two courses she told me that she would make it happen.

I met Leon in the first class of art, we hit it off. I did not hesitate to make acquaintances with others. Quickly, I found out that there were two distinct groups of students. One group that seemed to be the smaller of the two were the students that were born in the area. The second group that appeared to be much larger were the students that had moved from other states or other locations in Florida.

Those that moved from other states came to Florida to work at the Kennedy space center, the local air force base or several tech companies in the area, and those that were close to retirement and wanted to make the move early. It was easy making friends because most of us were new to the area.

One day Leon noticed that I looked a bit sad. I told him that I miss the water sports back in Panama City. To my shock he asked me if I had tried skim boarding or surfing. "Surfing, there is no surf in Florida.

As I chuckled, Leon asks if I could pick him up and drive him to Canaveral Pier. That Saturday, I was shocked to see a couple dozen of surfers catching and riding waves.

I don't remember exactly when or how, I managed to get a surf board and try it. On the north side of Canaveral pier, I managed to paddle in a wave, then stand up and ride it to shore, the very first time. I was hooked, hooked for life to that experience of riding a thing of excitement and beauty. That was the birth of a sport that I would be into for the next 50 years and would include my wife and children.

That next weekend, I took the two guns I got for Christmas years prior, sold them at a local gun shop for a great price. I was surprised that dad was glad to get rid of the guns and took me to the surf shop to purchase my first board. I had already bought a rack to place on the car to carry the board. I could not believe that dad was so nice for the first time ever. In reality nice to rid his home of the guns.

For a while mom was in a rehab hospital, dad and I would enjoy watching television shows together on weekends in our new environment. It seemed odd that we enjoyed the same stuff on television at that time. Ed Sullivan, Red Skelton, Bonanza were among our favorites And of course there was the Friday night fights.

We both laughed one night when they had an English group on the Beatles on the Ed Sullivan show. At that time, we made up a name for how they looked with that funny looking hair style, (the Nerd Girls). Another time on Ed Sullivan a group that I liked; the Beach Boys were on. Dad said he liked that group and the music was nice. New in town, I think dad was lonely just like me. During the year at school, I spent the majority of time with my friends while dad was with his new friends on the golf course. Crazy as it seems, when mom was in rehab, Dad and I got along well.

My brother was 9 at the time and we shared a large bedroom with an accordion type of divider that cut the room in half.

My focus on my life was surfing, I just could not get enough. Surfing was fun and provided a great escape from home. In that part of Florida, it was warm all year long with only spotty days where it would get cool.

There were certain places that did not have a sand bottom that made the waves more consistent due to the fact the bottom had a rock type coral called cokina rock. Sometimes it seemed like the whole senior class at school was at the same spot on the beach which made it feel like we were in one of those Frankie and Annette beach movies.

Making money with my art work was good as well. Leon and I worked together with our skills in art and some work in a local motel.

On Friday and Saturday evenings it was dancing at a teen club or going to a surf movie. Yet, there was still a longing for my girlfriend and friends back in Panama City and for the life I had there, and I was still bitter not being able to graduate with the friends I had since elementary school. Somehow, I will get back.

I HAD TO GO BACK – THINGS WERE NOT THE SAME – GOOD FRIENDS BACK IN MELBOURNE AREA.

School was out for the summer of 1964, I thought about taking a trip back to Panama City. My girlfriend had stopped writing me, and long-distance calls were expensive.

If I mentioned it to dad, I knew that he would be against it. Therefore, I took my surfboard to a friend to keep for me while I was gone. I was not sure how long I would stay. I had some money, but not much. I decided to hitch-hike. (Remember intrastate highways were just starting to be built). Late one afternoon a friend drove me to the edge of the county and let me out on a main road.

The first car stopped and a middle-aged man ask me where I was going, I told him Panama City Florida. He told me," I am going on highway 98 and going right by there." I believe God had directed that man, who knows where I might have wound up. When we arrived, he let me out next to a phone both to call my sister.

I stayed there a short time and had few chances to talk to my girlfriend. All other friends were busy with their lives, after all they had graduated. Things were not the same. Six months can make a big difference. The truth is the fact that you can't turn back the clock. It was a hard lesson for me to learn.

My ex-girlfriend's dad drove me back to the Melbourne area on his way to Miami to do some business. That was a blast because he had just bought a 1965 Mustang convertible. We rode all the way with the top down. That at least was some consolation.

All the way back to Melbourne, I wondered what the next few years would be like for me. I would be a senior in high school – then what next?

Back home, my parents did not say anything until the next morning dad simply said, "Did you get it out of your system?" I nodded a yes. Nothing else was said about that trip.

I went to a friend's house to pick up my surfboard and when I got there, several of my buddies were there waiting. "Come on Rick, lets catch some waves, a large eastern swell is coming in." *Wow, what a welcome, this was where I belonged.*

While back in the area I found out one of my friends from Panama City had moved to the area, his dad had just retired from the military. I knew immediately he needed to connect with us. He did, he even bought a surf board and learned to surf. The rest of the summer was surfing, movies and teen dances. The friends I had grown close to at that time, would be life lasting. The friends I left behind seemed to vanish in mind and heart.

A great sadness came, in just a few short years, three of these new friends would die in Vietnam, two would die in automobile accidents. One friend would struggle with the effects of agent orange.

One of those friends that was killed in Vietnam, would become very instrumental in my coming to Christ.

We boomers that served our country in this era, would be mocked and hated for service to our country. Many our age now look back at those good ole days with bitter sweet experiences. Our children and grandchildren would face a very different world with more wars mixed with national crisis from time to time. King Solomon was right, there is nothing new under the sun.

MY FULL SENIOR YEAR IS HERE, AND I WILL WALK THE LINE

Late August, I had to go to the administration office to schedule my semester. There I was told in order to walk the line in spring, that I would have to take some regular courses besides art. In order to do that I had to take a math and an English course, as well as a few other electives. By the end of the first semester, I was doing plenty of artwork for the school.

Before graduation, I was to design a simple stage for the graduation. The stage consisted of three white flames. A large flame in the middle represented our future, the far-left shorter flame represented our youth and the far right represented our retirement years looking back on our accomplishments.

This time would be the highlight of my grade school experiences. However, there were two obstacles looming in my mind. One was that fact that the elephant was back in the house making things extremely uncomfortable at home. The second was that I did not know what I wanted to do with my life other than art work and surfing.

Only in a few weeks and it would all be over. Our school annual came out and all had spent time signing and writing notes. To my surprise, many had written long drawn-out letters in my annual.

One particular classmate stood out. Irene, was a strong Christian girl and was not ashamed to speak about her faith. Many times, she told me she was concerned about me and my wild lifestyle and rebellious spirit. She told me that being a Christian can make a difference in my life. As I write this looking at her note in my high school annual, remembering times that we had talked, a warm feeling comes to mind of how a Christian that showed concern for a lost person can impact that person's life. Her life on earth was cut short... Jesus took her home. Later, I would be baptized in the same church that she attended.

The night of graduation, my sister had come down. Johnny, a dear friend was going to drive me because we had to be there early. My family would come later.

No! The elephant of alcoholism and mental illness would come to ruin it. Mom was going to ruin it for me. I was embarrassed for my friend Johnny to see her that way. It was so uncomfortable; I do not even want to write about it. Over the years, it had been a constant struggle to have an event focused on me from my own family.

Quickly, I asked Johnny to get me out of there. I don't remember if my family even came. Needless to say, I was upset making those old feelings of anger grow in me.

I did not go home after, rather I went to a friend's apartment where we were going to have a graduation party

The next morning, I went back to the house and like most all homes where the elephant walks, nobody said a word. My night of nights I wound away from my family.

When sis graduated, got married, when my little brother graduated kindergarten, all was fine. Me, my night to shine, showing off my design of the platform - all hell broke loose made by the elephant.

The Eau Gallie High School Commodores class of 1965 – Most all of us had been new to the area. We Leaned on each other in times of pain and rejoiced with each other in times to good. That school and the class of 65 will always be a highlight of life's experiences.

I learned from a teacher at school the strange *shotgun effect* after graduation. What would happen, in a very short time all those that were close to me, would scatter: some to college, some military, many would marry and start families and land careers.

I still think of those wonderful times and memories. The big plus was the fact that several of those gals I graduated with would continue to keep our class in contact over the years. I would be privileged to attend our 40th class reunion. Members of the class of 65 still meet from time to time back in Florida.

SUMMER – LIFEGUARD – COLLEGE.

After graduation, I approached dad about going to the local community college, that they had a great art program. I was interested because I was one of those rare students that got a scholarship in art for college. The amount was small. I asked

Dad to help me financially. He said if I wanted to go to college, I was on my own and he was not going to pay a single penny. I was not surprised, that seemed to be the norm. One positive thing later in life, I would feel like I did not owe may parents anything. Like the Sinatra song, "I did it my way."

That really bothered me; I was told for years he had sent money monthly to his daughter in Ohio from his first marriage and paid big money for my sister's wedding and had helped her schooling at Florida State. He paid to have my brother go to preschool and kindergarten.

My graduation present was a cheap camera, I am even embarrassed to say how much it cost let's just say I could have bought a bucket of chicken to feed the family lunch. From that point on I was on my own and nobody was ever going to tell me what I could and couldn't do and if there was a need for money, I would earn it.

From that day forward, I would do it all on my own. Dad was never again going to help me financially. Looking back, I through the years I had many jobs and made some good money for a kid my age.

I landed a job at the local swimming pool that summer after graduation; however, my lifeguard credentials had expired and I would have to become certified all over. At the pool that summer, I worked the cash register. On weekends the pool employees would work the local wrestling matches at the local gym operating the snack stand.

Along with that, I still made money doing artwork, that summer I made enough to pay for the fall and spring semesters. Mom was not allowed to drive and I was able to take her car to the community college; the round trip was about forty miles.

The government had started a link of intra state highways in the area. A section from the Melbourne area to Cocoa, Florida was opened we drove because it saved time.

A few of my high school buddies wanted me to go in with them to join a fraternity. Needless to say, it was fun; even the initiation and hazing. Afterward, it was more of the party life.

For me it got dull, there was an emptiness that did not ever get filled. I Still kept up with surfing, by this time I had bought a new long board that made my surfing experiences more exciting.

The summer of 66, surfing was sparce due to work and a lack of surf that summer. Got my credentials as a certified lifeguard, now, I was not at the cash register I was on the stand now.

Many times, folks would ask me if I had rescued anyone. There was one incident at the pool a preteen aged girl was struggling, I jumped in only to find the water shallow, I told her, just stand up, she did, to find herself in chest high water.

Another rescue was a friend while surfing was caught in a strong back wash. We both managed to swim parallel to the beach and let the waves push us in.

Later in Hawaii, I rescued a heavy-set tourist, who should have never been in the water that day. The surf was big, 8 to 10 feet and the currents were extra strong that day. As I was padding out that morning, he yelled to me for help. I managed to get him in with the help of another surfer.

The last one, my church had a college group come to work vacation Bible school one year. After the school was over, I took the group to a local waterfall. All of the group swam across the small pond at the base of the falls, while one stayed with me, a big guy who was a college football player. He finally stepped into the water going out about 20 feet or so into the pond when he yelled for help.

I knew the water was cold and that he might be cramping up. I thought If I go out, as big as he is we are both going to be in trouble. I found a dried-up log that was light and paddled out to him giving him the log to paddle himself back in. He thanked me, I told him that was our secret and nobody in the group were going to know.

At the end of the summer of 1966, I was asked if I would like to continue work for the city and work for the water department. The pay was great and the work... well, it was actually at the waste water treatment plant.

The work literally stunk but the pay was great. While I continued my college classes, I worked a day shift at the water department. At the end of the day the workers would gather would hang out a while before going home.

Two of the workers were strong committed Christian men. One man, Les, kept lovingly saying to me, "Just remember Rick, God has a plan for you, just turn to Christ and he will show you!" Those words one day would come to pass. Les was a fine man, and a great friend.

During those days the elephant was getting worse. I stayed as much as I could away from home. I felt for my brother. Dad did not make it better, "If you wouldn't be like you are, your mother wouldn't be like she is." I was the scapegoat for dad and mom's problems. This would continue until it came to an abrupt end and that was to come soon.

GIRLFRIEND AND HER FAMILY – GETTING MY OWN CAR

While working as a lifeguard at the pool, a cute girl lived close by the pool. When the pool closed in the evening, I would walk her home. I was struck by how much she seemed to care for me and how welcome I was hanging out at her home. It was great to be away from my home. I would stay as late as possible and not come home until all were asleep.

I was tired of driving mom's car; I know that is what dad wanted me to do to keep her from driving. However, I wanted my own car. It would be expensive for me unless I could put a car on Dad's insurance plan.

Dad. Told me, "As long as you're living under my roof you will never have your own car, your just too unreliable." Looking back, I know he wanted keep driving mom's car in order that she would not drive it.

At work I saw a station wagon that one of the guys had a sign on it for sale. The wagon was a 1956 Morris Minor wagon that was trimmed in real wood. Wow, the perfect "WOODY" surfer's vehicle! I pictured myself at all the hot surfing spots and how cool I would look driving up with my beach bunny surfer girlfriend. I asked him, "How much are you selling the wagon for?" Fifty dollars was the answer. I paid cash and drove it home. I was ready to buy my own insurance.

My life had been focused on life around water. During that day and time, you had three kinds of cool, you had the beach crowd, surfers, you had the bikers, especially Harleys and Indians, and you had the greasers, dirt track and drag strip. The coolest ride for the beach crowd was to have a station wagon and if your wagon was trimmed in real wood, you were a hit.

Driving home I noticed that my top speed was only 30 MPH and that *was going down a slopped road*. I did not know anything about cars at all except to drive them. At home, I opened the hood to see a shoebox size of a 4-cylinder engine. That had to be the smallest engine, I had ever seen. On top of that, the engine was smoking with obnoxious fumes.

I took the wagon to a foreign auto shop and talked with a mechanic there. He told me that was average size engine and it was designed for very small towns in Europe. He did tell me that he could order a larger engine. I asked how much; and he told me about six hundred dollars and it would take about four months before it could be shipped from England.

The next day I took the wagon back and gave to the man I bought it from and he gave me back my fifty. He did have another buyer for it. Would you believe years later that model was a classic and would sell well over ten thousand dollars (1970)

I went to my girlfriend's house that weekend and her sister found an ad that someone was selling a Chevy convertible, but it had a little rust.

We drove over and there was a 1961 Chevy Impala convertible, painted with gold paint and wire spoked wheels. I paid about three hundred dollars, thinking this is *so much cooler* than anything I could buy for that price.

I drove it home; dad had just got home. Looking at my car, dad did not say anything at all, but the look he gave me could melt iron. That summer and fall, I had the coolest ride I had ever rode.

Change was coming and everything was going to turn upside down. I never saw it coming. Years of struggling with family relationships. Being blamed for my mother's problems.

Parental favor towards my siblings. And, I had developed major problems with anger and trust issues that made me feel like a lone wolf, wild and out of control. Even some of my friends called me *the lone wolf,* funny some would call me "mule-skinner" because of my thick southern drawl.

NOBODY KNOWS THE TROUBLE I'VE SEEN - COMING MY WAY

It was September 7, 1967 my birthday. It was Friday, some of my co-workers at the water department wanted to take me to a local bar; I was of the official legal age to drink. That was fine because I knew I was not getting anything for my birthday other than a card from my sister.

There, they knew that I drank a beer now and then, but now it was going to be the hard stuff trying vodka, gin, and all kinds of whisky shots. Within a few hours I was so drunk I could not stand up on my own. As a surfer we did not drink the hard stuff because if the surf was up, you did not want to go out with a hangover.

Someone took me to the house and put me in mom's car. Sometime early that morning dad came out to mom's car' I had just awakened, when he grabbed me by my hair and slammed my head against the steering wheel and said, "You are a son of a bitch, you're going to be just like your mother!"

We never spoke a word to each other after that until October 11, 1967. It was over a month since my birthday. This was a day that was going to change everything in my life. That day it seemed as though my world was ending abruptly. Everything would finally come to a head.

Before going to work, I would always check the mailbox. Our house was usually the first house on our mailman's route. As I looked in there were three letters addressed to me. It was rare that I got any mail. As I looked those letters looked like something official was in them.

The first letter was from the community college I attended; it has stated that my core courses were failing even though my art classes were straight A's. Also in the letter, by law, they had to report this to my local draft board. That of course would immediately change my draft status.

The second letter was a company that did art for the Kennedy Space Center, they wanted to set up an interview. Good news at last I thought, I could work at the space center and make some good money. I could just imagine how great a career would be doing artwork for NASA.

Finally, the 3rd letter I opened was from the President of the United States, LBJ, stating that I had been selected by my draft board to report to duty that coming December 13th. Right before Christmas only a few weeks away.

That morning, I was called by my boss, upset that I had not shown up at work the day before. I thought I had told him that I had a test at school that day at school. The boss was very upset with me.

As I was walking toward my car dad stopped me, I did not say a word. The next thing he did was to continue to lay the blame of his problems with Mom on me again. He told me in a loud demanding voice," I want you out of this house by Saturday, you are making enough to be on your own and I don't want you around this house and stay away from your brother." I had heard that line so much over the years, was I danger to my brother? *Why did he kept saying that? Did I have leprosy? Was my brother one of those bubble boys?*

I got in my car without saying a word and left for work. Arriving there I did everything to avoid the boss. A co-worker asked me if I would help him do some work on his car that he drove on a dirt track each Saturday night. That was a good way to avoid going home.

My coworker was trying to weld a role bar into an old 56 Plymouth. We had a few beers then about 9:00 PM. I was feeling very bitter about the whole day completely forgetting that I had not contacted my girlfriend at all that day. We were engaged, I wanted to marry her and be a part of her family. My perception was her family was much better than mine, by the way they treated me.

I drove to my girlfriend's house only to see her dad standing at the door. "Not tonight, Rick, I don't want you around here right now." He was not angry but stern when he said that. That really hurt, I thought I could rely on him and his family.

I don't know if dad had called him but he seemed to know something was going on. As I left, something inside my mind had snapped.

I felt unwanted, unloved, and not needed. Feeling totally worthless to anybody I drove off fast. I wanted to leave every-thing behind, I wanted to end my pain of rejection as well as the anger and rage that grew inside me. I wanted to end it all... *What do I have to live for, after all, nobody wanted me?*

Driving down a boulevard well over a hundred miles an hour, I flew into palm trees that snapped like toothpicks. I did not even feel the impact shock. I kept driving knocking over several signs until the car stopped, engine smoking and steam pouring out the radiator.

I did not realize that I was out on a dead-end road. That was a symbol of my life a complete dead end. I even had failed to end it all.

I did not notice a policeman had been following me for the last couple of miles. I remember that he put his hand on my shoulder and said, "What's wrong son?" We struggled, hand-cuffed now I was in the back of the police car.

I think I blacked out, the next thing I remember is that I am in a paper suit laying on a bunk in a jail cell. Other inmates yelling, "Hey boy what did you do, rape the mayor's wife? Laughter filled the cell block until a guard told them to pipe down. Lights were dimed so the cellmates could sleep. I could not sleep. The cell I was in was designed just for one inmate. It was very small, Later I measured it to be a 4x6' foot cell.

I sat on the bunk a long time when something so strange happened, I thought my co-worker had given me a hallucinate drug in my beer.

There before my eyes was the face of Christ. It was the cru-cified face with thorns, blood and eyes that stared right at me. I would close my eyes it was still there. I said in a soft voice so others could not hear me," I have failed at everything in life, if you want my life, Jesus, you can have It, I don't care anymore. The vision of the face of Christ vanished.

Early that morning dad got me out. The only thing he said was that I was to have a court hearing soon. Nothing else was said. He dropped me off at the house.

It was silent around the house until mom came in to tell me she was going to have Mrs. Clark to come and talk to me.

Her son, Steve was the first person that friended me when I first attended Eau Gallie High School, her husband was friends with dad and her daughters were classmates in high school. I had a great respect for her. She was always soft spoken with a soothing voice.

Steve, her son, told me that our dads worked together and that if I needed anything he was there for me. I had a great respect for Steve. I even rode with him on *senior skip day* in 1964. He drove a car full of guys to San Orlando Springs. After his graduation Steve Joined the Marine Corps.

Steve's mom, Margret, told me they sent Steve home for a short R & R (that's what the military called it – rest and relaxation) His mom told me that Steve was bothered by something that had happened to him in Vietnam. Sadly, later, Steve would be killed in Vietnam after going back.

She told me a local pastor of a Baptist church helped Steve with his problems and that maybe that pastor could help me. She and her husband had been attending the church where the pastor was. That afternoon I had made an appointment with the Pastor, of Harbor City Baptist Church, the same church that my friend Irene had attended.

I was a bit nervous when I came into his office. After the formal introductions, He asked me, "What is your opinion about God?" "Oh, I believe there is a God, but most of the time we have to struggle with things on earth, "I continued with my perspective like many people that think they are Christian. "You know if your good outweighs your bad you will go to heaven, won't you?"

Gently, the pastor told me that it did not work that way and then he began to read me out of a booklet called the *Four Spiritual Laws*. I heard that God loved me and that he has a plan for my life, but sin has separated me from God and that my sin had to be delt with. I asked, "How in the world is that going to happen, I sin all the time." I thought there was no hope for me because of my sin. I wanted to know the plan that he had for me, but I felt like with my sin that would never happen.

Pastor answered, "That is right Rick, I think you already have a grasp on that issue. He continued to tell me that a righteous God had to punish mankind's sin and he did that through the crucifixion of Christ, his own son took the punishment for us and that faith in him and his sacrifice made it possible for eternal life to anyone who would just believe in Christ. The only dangerous sin, is the sin of rejection. It was then, that the vision in jail made sense to me. I knew how it felt to be rejected, I was not about to reject Jesus.

All these years I had continually felt rejected by my family and then God sent his son to die for me and all I have to do is repent and receive, and I would become a part of his eternal family. I had a lot to ponder after that visit with the pastor.

I told the pastor that I was going home and go over that booklet of the four spiritual laws. He told me to let him know what happens. From that day I attended Harbor City Baptist Church. One Sunday after receiving Christ into my heart, I went forward during invitation time to present myself to the church as a candidate for baptism and membership.

That same night I was baptized, Margret Clark and my mother came to my baptism. Both of them told me when I went into the water there was a glow on my face. From that day forward, I belonged to Christ. The next few weeks until my induction into the army, I attended the evening services.

I had my court hearing and was to serve my time from 6 pm on Friday evenings to 4 pm on Sunday evenings, doing janitor duties at City Hall and the police department until the day I was to be inducted in the Army. If I finished my work the officer in charge would let me go home early for evening services at church.

The judge cleared my record so that I might have a better military experience with no criminal record. There is no record of that event other than this book. God began to become a central focus of my life. However, I needed to grow spiritually. That too would come much later in life. From then on, there was no doubt of my salvation through Christ.

YOUR IN THE ARMY NOW AND NOT ON A SURFBOARD

Dad drove me to the bus station in Titusville, all he said to me when he let me out in a group of other young me, "Be a man, take whatever they do to you as a learning, don't fight back or argue."

The induction center was in Jacksonville Florida. Much of the day there was spent going through medical testing. For me I was medically fit, due to surfing and lifeguard training.

It was embarrassing because, we had to disrobe down to only our underpants. There were female nurses and doctors all over. One young man did not have any underwear, they finally gave him a towel to wear.

I became hysterical when we were told to line up in the hallway, face the wall and bend over spreading your cheeks. The doctor would walk down both sides of the wall checking for hemorrhoids. What made it funny was you were looking at the guys across from you and they were looking at you. Several, including myself laughed out loud.

The induction was over when a major came in and said that we would be staying at a hotel in downtown Jacksonville. He also told us we were free to do what we wanted and we had to be at the lobby not one second late at 10 am for the bus to pick us up to carry us to Fort Benning, Georgia.

A chaplain came in to tell us that when we get to Fort Benning that we would surrender all our possessions and that the possessions would be mailed back to our home. Then he told us chilling information that about one third of us would not go home any sooner than 18 months. He went on to tell us that we will spend 8 weeks in boot camp and that if we did not pass requirements that we would take boot camp all over from the beginning. Then he told us that our time would be shorter if after boot camp and advanced training, if we were sent to Vietnam our time in military service would be shortened.

A guy standing next to me whispered, "Yea, in a body bag.!"

That evening in downtown Jacksonville almost all of those men went out on the town. A great economy thrust to down-town Jacksonville, all kinds of establishments we opened catering to service men. I went out with the other 3 guys that shared a room with me. We went to a "GO-GO" bar. That is where girls in short tasseled dresses, danced in cages and for a tip they would dance on your table.

One of the guys wanted to go to another place. I wanted to finish my drink. The girl dancing in the cage next to us took a break and sat down at my table. She told me. "You look like a nice guy; do you mind if I sit here to take my break?" I told her it was ok.

We talked. She showed photos of two children and that her husband was in Vietnam. She had to dance to make ends meet. I told her I understood and gave her a tip. I had taken cash from my last 2 months of pay not knowing what I would need.

In the years ahead there would be many like her and many that would never see their husbands again.

Some would be former classmates in Melbourne and Panama City. I counted about 26 one time on the memorial wall that I knew.

All of us got on the bus mid-morning heading for Ft Benning. It was late by the time we got to the base; they had put us up in a barracks that was so old, we saw a small carving on a door jamb that said, SW 1930.

The next day we were told to disrobe all of our civilian clothing. We went to a warehouse in a long single line. Each station we were given items, the first was a large duffle bag with our names and military I.D. number already stamped on the bag. After going through getting all the gear, we were quickly measured to receive our dress uniforms.

We were told to put on our fatigues, cap and boots. For the next couple of days, it seemed like we were going from orientation to orientation. Most of it was watching movies. The movies about STD were had most all of us laughing because they were showing the after effects on soldiers mostly from WWII. I felt sorry for those guys.

Great news that day, many of the staff in the boot camp were taking off for Christmas. We had the opportunity to take off for that Christmas and go home but we only could take five days and you had to have your own money for bus fare. Most stayed, they had not brought any money.

I had enough money and I had my dress uniform on. I was shuttled to a bus terminal and took the bus back to Melbourne.

At home, all were surprised. I am glad I did not stay long the elephant was back in the house. I felt for my brother who had to stay in that home. I did get to spend a time with my girlfriend, at that time I thought things were fine in our relationship. After two days, I headed back.

On the way back to Fort Benning, I began to think about my parents and where they were spiritually. I had never prayed for my parents because I felt disgusted by the way they seemed to focus negative attention on whatever I did. There was a point that I had given up trying to get their attention in a positive way.

From the Florida/Georgia border to Columbus. Georgia. I prayed for them. Being a very young Christian now my prayer was more like going over the past years. I did not know that in the next few years my life would continually make more radically changes.

The eight weeks at boot camp were fun, although many hated it. I took boot camp to be like a hazing but with purpose. The captain of our company came up to me and told me that he wished all his men in training had my kind to attitude. I was actually having fun.

I remembered when Elvis was drafted, he proudly served his country whereas other celebrities did what that could to avoid the draft. Boot camp was fun!

I was disappointed because soldiers every now and then had to do K.P. I was looking forward to peeling potatoes and washing pots and pans just like you see in the movies. I was told that day, that I would be a server on the chow line and police the area ... bummer!

I was surprised that the physical aspect of training did not affect me as much as it did others; I attribute that to the fact that my surfing and beach life had kept me fit.

Yet, as I remember this experience there was one thing that bothered me more than anything. Each day at mail call most of the guys would get mail and packages. It seemed that those that said they would write me, did not. I did get one letter from dad, a couple from my sister, Including a package with cookies.

I felt abandoned, but the worse would come in my 4th week at boot camp. I go the infamous "Dear John" letter. Even the church I was baptized in was going to send me their weekly bulletins did not. I was upset. I had enough change to call my girlfriend only to get the silent treatment.

Sundays we were allowed to go to chapel service, both in the morning and the evening services. That helped some. The chaplain, would mention that if anyone needed to talk, we could make an appointment with him after our duty hours (mostly on Sundays).

I noted that my biggest problem was the built-up anger, and a new one being developed was issues with trust; I no longer could trust anyone. Trust issues would only worsen with time.

I took my problems to the chaplain. I told him I needed to get stronger in my faith. He told me that I might consider becoming a chaplain's assistant. I thought that was a great idea and he put a recommendation in for me to get chaplain assistant's training right after boot camp.

On the last day of training, we had to be timed going through a long obstacle course. It was very cold and raining the whole day at the course. Sometimes the rain would turn to snow or sleet. What made it worse was the fact that all of our clothing was saturated with cold mud. We were all exhausted by the time we got back to the barracks. I went to my bunk and crashed; not even go to mess hall for dinner.

I awoke the next morning and had to be helped to sick bay. I had a 104-degree temperature and was coughing up blood.

Within minutes a truck made to be a type of ambulance came to pick me up. The staff took off my fatigues, put an IV in me and placed me in a ward. By that time, I was in and out of consciousness.

Late the next morning doctors went back and forth, not saying anything to me while checking me. When I asked, they would respond with, "Your superior officer will inform you when he comes in."

At noon my company captain came in with some magazines and a newspaper. "Watkins, you were great on the obstacle course, you made us proud, I think you came in 3rd with your time out of the three companies." The captain continued, "I have to tell you that you have been diagnosed as having upper respiratory infection in both lungs. Civilians would call that double pneumonia; I will be by each day to check on you." I responded with a faintly, "Thank you sir."

My stay at the hospital for just over two weeks; thankful for reading material my captain gave me. It frightened me most when I coughed up blood. When I was ready to be released, my captain drove his personal car to pick me up to carry me back to the barracks.

Everyone was gone, they had graduated boot camp and had gone on to advanced training only staff remained behind. I had to wait a few more days to have new orders cut for chaplain's assistance school in Fort Dix, New Jersey. In the meantime, I did light duty around the office and mess hall of our company.

Finally, my orders came in for Fort Dix New Jersey.

Catching a bus to the Atlanta airport I got a flight to New York. As the plane began to descend, looking out the window frightened me. There was nothing but continuous city all the way to the horizon. I thought, "How in the world am I supposed to find Fort Dix in all of that!"

To my relief, military greeters were there to meet soldiers coming in from all over to take military trucks to Fort Dix and other places in the area. For me that was great.

There on the truck, I had met several from Florida and one from Georgia. As we talked, all of us were going to chaplain's Assistant school, comrades in faith! These guys would help me to grow further in my faith. We were all boomers, our fathers served in WWII and I think 2 fathers had been veterans of the Korean war.

Arriving at the fort we went straight to the barracks assigned to us and slept the night. The next day a sergeant came in looking for me.

Given the information that the position for chaplain's assistant that I was to fill had to be filled and that I would be placed in the Administration school. Needless to say, *wow*, greatly disappointed not knowing what I would be doing or where I might be going.

The administration school was not bad and that it was more like going to an office and working – nine to five! At orientation we went to we were told of all the things that were available to us when we were not on duty or training.

This was a great place. A chapel was right next to our barracks and was open 24/7 – some of the guys in the chaplain's assistant school gathered for fellowship and singing, playing the piano and organ. (That was encouraged for those that would be chaplain assistants.)

Alone on weekday evenings, I spent after hours at the recreation center just down the street. The urge to create works of art was spurred on at the center. Drawing portraits for many of my buddies of their wives and children. They paid me ten dollars for a penciled drawing. I did some other drawings of silly cartoons. Doing that, made time go by fast giving me peace of mind.

One day a sergeant came into the Administration school and asked. "I was told there is a cartoonist and portrait drawer in this class." At once, all the guys in class including a lieutenant pointed toward me. "Come with me private, we've got some work for you." The sergeant said with a relieved smile on his face.

He told me that they were working on slides for trainees that were going into supply operations school. He asked if I could draw cartoons and that he would give me the ideas of what he wanted then they would take photos of the cartoons and make slides out of them. This gave me a great amount of freedom and a lot of clout with the staff. I spent more time drawing cartoons for slides than I did in Admin. School.

Once a week we had physical training, sometimes they let us play tag football. I must have gotten dehydrated one day and got a kidney infection. Another time I sprained my right foot and was on crutches for a couple of weeks.

During the stay at Ft. Dix almost every weekend, I went into Philadelphia and stayed at the YMCA downtown. Many times, those buddies from the chaplain's school went with me. Often, we would go to the salvation army for services on Sunday before heading back to base. If you were in uniform, everything was free, movies – museums- the Zoo and big discounts at eating establishments. I loved the city there.

One weekend something strange had happened. It was a weekend early in April that year. I got an early pass to go to Philly on that weekend. Very strange coming into town there was very little traffic. When I arrived at the YMCA the recep-tionist told me that all military passes were canceled. Then, I found out that Martin Luther King had been assassinated. She told me to wait and that a person from the salvation army would drive me back to the base.

I finally got orders for my military assignment. I was to report back to Fort Benning to work as an administration clerk for the infantry school. I had two weeks before I had to report so I went home to Melbourne, to see some friends and catch some waves.

WHY DID I EVEN COME HOME – BACK TO BENNING.

Mom and dad were surprised to see me. Going in my bed-room, I was shocked, my surf board was gone, it had been stolen is what I was told. How could it be stolen since I kept it in my bedroom.

Most items of my clothing and personal belongings such as photos, a few of my art pieces. All of my nick knacks that guys have including my coin collection gone, that alone was worth hundreds of dollars. One coin alone was worth $200.00. All my books and surfing magazines were gone. I had three photo books of WWII and Korea; they were gone with an entire set of encyclopedias.

Asking dad," where is my stuff?" He shrugged his shoul-ders. Turning to my little brother who was about thirteen at that time. He did the same as dad. To this day, no answer had been given. How does that stuff just disappear from a man's bedroom?? It was like I had never lived in that house, like they were trying to erase my existence from the family.

At least I had left some of my art work with my ex-girlfriend. I went to her house to retrieve my art work. Can you believe, even that was gone? Years later I was told she sold for drug money. It was nice to know people would pay for my work.

I decided to get with my friends especially some of my surfing buddies. All of them were gone, military, college, marriage, whatever. I had about just a few more days when I got a call from my ex-girlfriend, the one that had sold my art work. She asked me, "Why didn't you call."

For a very short time I thought she might want to get back but when I saw her, I knew it was not going to happen she had become big time in the Hippie scene and was into drugs. The drug and hippie scene were not my thing.

My good friend Johnny had a job at a surf shop. I called him, he said those magic words, *hey, let's go surfing*. I will loan you a board. To a great discomfort, short boards were the craze. Long boarding was out. Those that rode the short board were ripping the waves to shreds. Heartbroken, that was the best way to describe my feelings.

From the time I got home, I wanted to get back to Benning. That coming home was a total disaster. Needless to say, anger and now major trust issues were welling up again. I could not trust my family to take care of my stuff. It was like I had never lived in that house or town. I could not get back to Benning fast enough. I felt like I was never going to experience the love of a real family. Mine had all but deserted me erasing me out of their lives.

BACK AT BENNING – AIR BOURNE SCHOOL – BUT NOT JUMPING

Fort Benning was a fine place to be stationed, before long I had good friends. It seems like everywhere you went it was easy making friends because all of us were lonely.

The barracks were comfortable there was only a few of us and it was easy to make it look like home. My window looked out at a boxing ring. A ringside view on weekends of matches between soldiers in the Airborne School was entertaining. The day room had color television and a pool table. Everything I needed was in walking distance. I had plenty of time to do artwork and give it away to good buddies of mine.

Our unit had special guard duty on the base. We would do guard duty at the Infantry Museum. Our job was to walk around, especially when visitors were there, due to the fact there were valuable historical items. It was never boring looking at the history of the U.S. Infantry. I was surprised to see a display on the 70th infantry where my father had been. At least that guard duty was interesting. It felt good just to be back in Georgia.

As a believer in Christ like many in the Bible belt, you get saved then after that you're on your own. Later in life I would see this happen to many. The attitude I developed was, that I didn't care anymore. I started back drinking and even started smoking. I still did not care to use curse words.

Much later I would discover that I was judging God by the actions of how people treated me. Forgetting that people have choices. I was a baby Christian that did not want to grow or change, I was angry at everything even though I was blind to how good I had it, even in the army. Nobody was going to get may mailing address; I did not care about mail any longer. Spending almost a year, I could count the mail received on one hand plus one birthday card. (Six pieces of mail) Where as many of my comrades were getting regular mail almost daily.

My joking around and doing artwork made me popular with my comrades. Being invited to go places with the guys. I had a great time in Fort Benning. Hanging around the joints in Columbus Georgia. Was fun. A bunch of us even went to the local fair. That brought back memories of the awards won with my art work at the county fairs in Florida. We all went to the Hoocheechoochee show at the fair only to see a much older woman dance in a skimpy outfit, it was like your mother dancing in a skimpy outfit in front of your friends.

Late that summer our office captain requested me to come to his office. He addressed me," Rick, you have been a real morale booster around the office and with the men, but I have some news, some orders came down for your next assignment. It looks like you will be in Vietnam very soon." He told me to start making plans and that I could take leave or go straight to my assigned duty.

Not bothered by the idea of going to Vietnam, I was more bothered by the thought that nobody would really care. I told the captain that I would take 3 weeks to go home. To get some go surfing in.

A couple of days later, the captain called me in again telling me the Vietnam orders had been superseded by new orders involved going on a special assignment and that I would have to have a top-secret clearance and that it would take about twenty to thirty days.

I was flabbergasted. "SAY WHAT!"

The next duty was going to wind up in Seoul Korea attached to the Eighth Army Headquarters. The orders came and I was off to go back home for a short stay, then to Fort Lewis Washington, then on to Korea.

My captain asked, "Do you know someone in the pentagon?" I did not know anyone at that time, but later when I got out of the army, I found out a relative, Mom's sister, worked in the Pentagon. At that time, she was a GS13. Years later she told me she was tired of our family members going to war and she had some control and clout in the Pentagon. I believe that God had made all of this happen. Later in life, I could see how this would all work out for His will in my life in my spiritual pilgrimage, for now, I was still facing perils.

After staying home, a couple of days, I booked a flight to Seattle, then took a shuttle to Fort Lewis. When I arrived, I stayed in a nice more modern barracks than that of Fort Benning. I was told it might a while before I get a flight, that they had to wait for my clearance to be finished. I stayed there for 2 weeks watching television and shooting pool. It actually became very boring to me.

KOREA – EASY JOB, BUT BORING – DRINKING TOO MUCH

The day arrived to fly to Korea via Japan. The plane was packed with soldiers. We all had our dress uniforms on. Most got off the plane in Japan. I found out they were going to Vietnam.

Getting off the plane in Korea, there were two armed soldiers there to meet me. It was mid-November we took a long cold ride to 8th Army headquarters in an open-air jeep. I noticed all the other soldiers took buses. My escorts told me that due to my security clearance, I had to be escorted.

The road was dusty and it was very cold, my mustache had ice on it. I saw many Koreans living in drainage pipes. When we got to Seoul, I also notice that a few roads were paved but most were still dirt. Everything was so dusty.

Korea has radically changed since then. After being there for thirteen months I made a judgment call that one day this country would rise up and become a great power, economically. Yes, it did come to pass.

I was given a three-day period in a small building to adjust to the time. I was also visited by a soldier from the unit I was going to work with. Once again, due to my late arrival the position I was to do to have had been filled, however, due to my clearance, I would be assigned to the 8TH Army Headquarters Administration office.

Some of the work was classified, but the rest of the work was easy and even on the brink of boring. Off hour times were getting acquainted with others.

The living quarters were fantastic. The room was shared with two American GI's and one Korean soldier. This was done this in order that we could learn and appreciate each other's language and culture.

Just two buildings down, there was a club for enlisted men. I would spend much of my free time drinking and gambling. Some weekends I was so drunk that I would sleep through Saturday and wake up Sunday with a headache.

One day one of my coworkers told me that I might on the verge of becoming an alcoholic. That shocked me into thinking that I did not want to end up like mom back home. The thought of that horrified me, but had an admiration for his concern, someone cared.

A few days later we had to qualify again with our weapons, the M14 rifle and the side arm pistols. At the gun range they had set us up alphabetically. Winding up in the last trench and they did not have enough ear plugs for all. We shot our weapons until sunset. By that time my ears started ringing and continued for several weeks.

Upon my release from active service, test showed damage in my right ear. Back in the USA, contact was made by a veteran's hospital in Miami. After a trip to Miami being tested at the VA hospital, they told me there was nothing they could do, but to claim any disability, there would need to have proof that there were no extra ear plugs. Of course, that would be impossible to prove. Same ole government bull!

Gene, my co-worker and I would talk a lot, we even became good friends. Gene encouraged me to spend more time at the USO club. We both did. Drinking had stopped all together, but still smoked too much.

I spent so much time at the USO, that the staff used me as a speaker at various events and games. Public speaking seemed to come natural to me, not realizing God would be using that gift of gab. Gene and the USO club were to change my outlook on life.

Gene was also a Christian, but a back slider. Not knowing what that was, he told me and that described me to perfection. Going to chapel services was not that great most of the services were ecumenical and somewhat dull.

During that time, dances were held at the USO, though there were not so many ladies to dance with, often Korean girls from the Women's University of Seoul would volunteer to come to dance with the guys in order to practice their English.

One day I met this Korean girl that spoke almost perfect English and a couple of other languages. To make it short, after seeing her on a regular basis, I did wind up marrying her. I thought her love was real. Her mother had been an actress in Korean television and movies. The wedding we had was like *Who's Who* in the Korean entertainment business.

I was invited by her mother to visit a Buddhist temple. As I sat outside and not going in the temple, even as a baby Christian, I did not feel right about it. Later, food had been prepared for us. I still, but politely declined the offered food. Years later, the mother became a very devout Christian. I was told by her that she admired my convictions at the temple in Korea.

Before we got married, my fiancée had to go through a thorough background check due to the clearance and work I was doing. After a few short years, we divorced. That story will come later.

Very little mail came to me during my stay. Once again, all those that said they would write, did not. One day I did get a letter from my ex-girlfriend's mother.

Somehow, she had got the word that I was going to marry. She must have got that from my parents along with my mailing address. I did not give the address to anyone but somehow my parents obtained it.

In the letter she was upset that I was getting married and that I should give my ex-girlfriend another chance. But I had found out that she was still sowing her wild oats, that happened before I even left home to deploy to Korea. She wound up doing some time in jail for drugs.

Once again, my spiritual focus dimed. Later, finding out that if I had been closer to God much of my heartache and frustration would not have happened. I know that I had to experience what I went through to get close to him.

Homeward Bound – Starting Over – I Can't Get No Satisfaction

Active service time was over. That meant doing time in the Army reserve and the unit I would be attached to would notify me.

Arriving at home now with a wife at hand, we had to stay with my parents and brother a short time until I could fine us a place. Immediately, it was very uncomfortable for all of us. I had started to look for a furnished apartment to live. I also had to get a car. Dad told me I could use mom's car.

By law I was entitled to go back to my job with the water department. A big change had occurred while, both the City of Melbourne and the smaller city of Eau Gallie had united into one city. Everything was different, but in a good positive way. I worked in the main office for a while because of my management skills learned in the army. I also did plenty of drafting for the department.

The office was near to where my parents lived, so I could check on mom and my wife. There was a lot of friction between those two. In less than a month I had my own car and a furnished apartment to live in.

The first Sunday at home, my wife and I went to church; the same church that I had received Christ and was baptized. Baptist at that time would separate men's and women's Sunday school classes.

I did not attend the men's class. The pastor wanted me to teach a boy's class of 12-year-old boys. I was hesitant, but the pastor knew that by my teaching that I would be learning as well. Teaching that class aided my learning more about the Bible than I did reading that Good News paperback in the Army. Teaching had a special enjoyment there is a great satisfaction to see young boys enlightened with new knowledge from your efforts while I was becoming enlightened having to study in preparation.

After a few weeks the pastor wanted me to go on visitation with the church leaders. I continued to do this for a good while learning much about how to talk to people about Christ; but, was still shy about doing that. One visitation event was to minister to guys in the city jail, the same place I was incarcerated in over two years back. It felt strange, but I gave a brief testimony.

My wife, began to openly share with a few of the ladies of the church. One of the ladies came to me to tell me what my wife had requested.

Shocked to find out that she wanted to have an abortion my response was, "no way." In Korea abortions were legal; surprised that in Korea she had and abortions without my knowledge.

I shared this situation with those Christian men at the water department. Les told me to buy a house, maybe that way she would feel more stable having our own place.

With the help of Les and others, soon we were able to have a custom home built on the government's 235 program. Within a few short months, a 3-bedroom, bath and half home became ready for us to move in.

Several buddies in the water department helped me to furnish the house. A thrift shop to provide some low-cost kitchen items. We moved in. Dad gave me an old black and white tv with rabbit ears that was able to get about 3 channels. It was like I had accomplished the American dream. And yet, it seemed that was not enough to satisfy my wife. There was nothing but friction in the home.

That first summer back in Florida, orders came to do my reserve duty back at Fort Benning that summer, glad because I was familiar with Benning and the work going to be doing was back in the Infantry school. There awaiting me was a big surprise.

The unit I was attached to was based in Panama City Florida. The captain, the superior officer, was my science teacher in high school and all but a few of the unit had been classmates in school. Those three weeks were great! It was like a mini class reunion with classmates.

The work was simple I had to file military records. I worked in a large room by myself with a radio going much of the time. The work was completed the first two weeks. I had filed alphabetically thousands of military records. At the end of the three weeks, I received a letter of commendation noting that the work I did in two weeks was what it would take ten men to do in that same time frame. Sometimes working alone, you can accomplish much more with little effort, just steady focus on the job.

During the time I was away, my wife had come in contact with two Korean ladies that lived in Melbourne. One Korean lady was a strong Christian her husband was a commercial fisherman. The other lady lived in a fine house off the Indian River. Her husband, I believe worked as an engineer in a local firm.

For a while it seemed to satisfy her. Yet, spite all that, we still were not getting along. Each day living in that house created drama. My thought was to ignore it thinking it was due to the pregnancy and maybe knowing that she could not get an abortion.

It was in February that my first child was born. Stephanie, my daughter, was the apple of my eye bringing immense joy having her. Every moment of the day my desire was to be with her. I would watch her at night while my wife worked at restaurant. She would watch her during the day.

One evening when it got bad between my wife and I, I called her Sunday school teacher to come over to settle her down. I drove off so that they could have some privacy.

Coming back, her Sunday school teacher told me that to let her go. "What do you mean?", I asked. Her teacher told me that she had never loved me. I also learned that the well to do Korean lady had a fancy restaurant in Hawaii and that my wife wanted to move there and work for her. She was told she could make a lot of cash. Money and wealth seemed to be the only focus my wife had.

Hawaii – Not for Long

Knowing that if she was not satisfied living in Florida that I could go to Hawaii and check it out. I found out that I had all my vacation days that was never taken before I went in the army. My wife had been working as a waitress at the local Holiday Inn and had saved a lot of money, off to Hawaii now, I hope she will be satisfied.

When we arrived, we took a cab to a local hotel in Waikiki. Contact was made with the Korean lady from Florida. She had arrived there weeks earlier.

My wife started working the first night there while I sat with my daughter. My stay was short, quickly back to Florida to sell the house and drive the car across country to ship it to Hawaii. My wife had told me that she was never going back no matter what; Hawaii was going to be her home from then on.

While taking a flight back to Florida to sell the house and move to Hawaii. I was ready to give up all to satisfy my wife and have a family. The desire to have a family; at that point made me willing to do anything to get it. I was willing to do anything to make a family for myself Feeling that the way I had been treated by my family. I was determined to have my own no matter what the cost.

Selling the home now was a single man task. I had massive garage sales. It was a bitter heart-breaking experience with all the energy and struggles to get the house, and in a short time giving it all up. I felt embarrassed that my coworkers had help me to obtain all that I had to give it all up in a very short time.

My real-estate agent told me to get the house super clean and repair anything that needs it because he could get a better price for me. The agent did make some profit, selling the home.

The plan was, to drive my car across country, ship it to Hawaii then fly myself over. As I drove across the country, the anger and trust issues began to come back asking myself, "Why am I leaving everything and for what" Of course the answer was my baby girl. I wanted my own family and give them what I never got from my family.

A good friend drove with me, he wanted to see if he could secure a job in Hawaii. Our stay was very short.

One afternoon, my wife was getting ready for work when I noticed a see-through blouse she was wearing with a skimpy laced bra. I blew my top and we had a big fight. Wearing that was supposed to get her bigger tips at the restaurant. My friend left me. I glad he did that was so embarrassing.

A few days later my wife came to an agreement, that if I landed a high paying job back in the mainland, she would come back to me. She had no intentions of ever getting back *with* me. Her agreement was only to get rid of me. Rejection, anger, and trust issues pushed out all the accomplishments made up until that time. I felt so unloved.

Back To Florida Again – Job Hunting

Back at the house with my folks. Dad, for the first time, was very sympathetic towards me. He kept telling me how sorry he was that I wound up in this situation. I think he was reflecting what he went through when he lost his daughter from his first marriage. It was much of what I was going through. In a strange way it seemed to bond us together closer than we had ever been.

He knew a lot of people in a lot of places and set up a job interview back in Panama City Florida with the water department. I believe those that hired me had owed my dad for their jobs when he was the city manager there several years back.

Years, back in Melbourne, I had taken some courses and passed to get my state licenses in water and waste water management along with over several years of experience.

At first, thinking that would be great landing a job there in my old stomping grounds but, that would not work out.

That job was very short- lived. Working for the water department there, I never got a job description, I just hung around an office all day with nothing to do. I resigned and started looking on my own.

Landing a great job in a city in the northern part of eastern Florida. I went back to Melbourne to get ready. Eagerness to look forward to a better life and a family.

I did not know that God was about to do something that would radically change everything. Going back to Melbourne with great expectations that great things were going to happen. Great things did happen but not in the way I expected, God had a whole different plan for me. When God has his plan for you, things are going to happen unexpectedly.

Encounter With the Holy Spirit – I Needed to grow

I picked a book at a local book store. The topic of the book was about being filled and empowered by the Holy Spirit. The book used a term I had never heard of other than the Bible.

That term was *being baptized in the Holy Spirit* and that many during the Jesus movement had experienced this phenomenon with evidences that followed by receiving spiritual gifts mentioned in the New Testament. Baptist would use the term, *being filled*. I believe it does not matter the term used, the important thing is to be empowered to live and serve. *Read Matthew 3: 11*

The more I read, the more I knew this would be something that could change my life, becoming empowered to live a better life. That was what was needed and that is what I wanted. I needed power to live with spiritual confidence and assurance.

The few times, reading the New Testament of the Bible, when it mentioned the Holy Spirit, I was taught in Baptist churches that it was only back then for the early church to get started. Yet, the book I read told of how it had empowered the writer and many others, it was for the here and now.

The thought came to me, "Who is man that places limits on what God can do or cannot do." Isn't he the same yesterday, today and tomorrow? How can mere man accept some things of God, limit other things? Where did they come up with the idea that God does not work that way anymore? These questions that came to my mind would open the door to a new experience with God.

That is what was needed and that is what I wanted. In three days, I would be in San Francisco to meet my wife and daughter. We would drive across the country back to Florida. A new start was something I wanted and now something to empower me for a better life and experience with God. I stayed at my parents in Melbourne' after the interview with a new job.

It was a Sunday about nine in the evening when I strolled down to an elementary school near the house. I sat in a swing and started praying. When I asked for the Holy Spirit to be in my life, I was afraid of getting zapped, because in the book I read the author mentioned that he had started to pray in tongues.

I tightened up thinking I was going to get zapped. Nothing happened. Then I prayed again, "Lord I am going to ask one more time, and this time I am going to believe that you are going to give me your Holy Spirit baptism, and if anyone asked me, I am going to tell them that I have the baptism of the Holy Spirit of God in my life!" Not knowing much about theology at that time, I believed with the faith I demonstrated, a response came.

God began speaking to me in my mind and heart, and I know that it was Him speaking, telling me that I needed to learn more about him and his word and that he would guide me.

Walking back to my parent's house I had felt a strange sense of peace about everything, not knowing that a storm was about to hit. God's timing is perfect even when we fail him.

I read some then fell asleep. About 4:30 AM, Dad came into the room to wake me. "Rick you wife is on the phone" I picked up the phone and she said, "I am not going to meet you, I am going to divorce you and you will never see me or your daughter again!"

Before I had a chance to speak, she hung up. Strange, but I still had the peace that God was in control and that I just had to trust him. I felt that He was the only one to trust, all others failed me. Somehow it felt different now that the Holy Spirit was a part of my life.

I did not go back to sleep. Later that morning, Mrs. Clark had heard what happened and brought me a book to read, '*Prison to Praise*" by Merlin R. Carothers. It was just what I needed.

I need to praise and thank God no matter what happens, and I did. I praised him for his goodness and for the trials that I had gone through. Now grasping an understanding of how these things had strengthened me over time I had a better understanding of how God uses circumstances to make you grow if you focus on Him.

As I look back at these events in my life, I see it now clearly it is a spiritual pilgrimage, yes, a spiritual pilgrimage of a true southern baby boomer going through the perils of life.

I notified the town that had hired me that some radical changes had occurred and they needed to find someone else. They were sorry but thanked me for some suggestions to fix a problem with one of their waste water treatment plants.

Planning to Return to Hawaii – Leaving with Peace in My Heart

Doing some research, in order to obtain a divorce, in Hawaii, you had to prove malice otherwise, it was a two-year wait. (Of course, laws have changed in the last 50 years.) I would return to Hawaii, get a job and establish myself so I could get visitation rights with my daughter. She was the apple of my eye. From then on, my focus was her and the empowerment of God's spirit. Little did I realize at that time God intended me to live my life in Hawaii serving him.

My next task was to get some financial resources to help me. That is when many miracles began to happen. My income tax return check came in the very next day, then Dad told me that Papaw was coming down to see me and was going to help me financially. And the profit I had selling the house.

By the time I was ready to leave I had more than enough to go, until I could find employment, even if I had to wash dishes or dig ditches, this time, I was staying in Hawaii.

About to visit some friends the Saturday before leaving that Tuesday, when Papaw Watkins told me to stay home, because he was going to talk to Mom and dad; he wanted to get them to worship with me that Sunday because I would be leaving that Tuesday to return to Hawaii.

He told me, "Let's make sure we get them there." That meant we had to sober them up. We had to make them promise to go with us. That was not an easy task, after years of excuses and neglect.

Both of my parents had been active in churches when they were young. Dad shared with me; at one time he was the choir director in a church in Dalton. Mom was active in the church in Nicklesville in her youth.

That Sunday, the church was full; that was normal for Harbor City Baptist. We four sat in the back. As the sermon was over, Papaw told me to go down and pray at invitation time.

I was down at the prayer alter on my knees, when I heard Papaw praising the Lord very loudly. I was thinking, Papaw, this is a Baptist church not the church of the Nazarene.

At that moment, I felt a hand on my shoulder, it was Mom on her knees, looking to my right was Dad on his knees. I began to weep.

I know that they had been active in church years ago in their youth. Yet, they wanted to be baptized that night together. I had the privilege to see them baptized together. Over the years to come they were active in the church until aging and physical problems set them in a retirement medical care home.

While in good health they worked with the church helping former alcoholics. Needless to say, my attitude towards them was beginning to heal. Peace and a new relationship flourished with them. The past was the past, all things are new now. I am totally on my own with God.

That Tuesday boarding the plane in Melbourne, would the last time I would see Papaw in this world. I kept wonderful memories of our talks. I know that I will see him again with eternal joy. Thank you, heavenly father for my granddaddy. A joy with the peace and power of God's spirit was growing inside me.

Deep Thoughts in Flight – New Start – New Church

Before leaving Melbourne, there was no attempt to pack much, knowing I would not need much needed living in Hawaii. On the flight, I reflected back to my youth at Maude and J.L.'s home looking at the View Master of all the Hawaiian slides and in grammar school reading stories of Hawaii, never realizing that Hawaii would become my permanent home.

God must have been preparing me, when I was young. I was thinking, even surfing I will be living where surfing started.

Before the flight from Los Angles to Honolulu an announcement in the waiting room warned the group traveling that all hotels were booked solid and if we did not have reservations, they would provide information how to get their money back.

Nothing was about to stop me, even if I had to stay on a park bench, God had brought me this far and I was not going back.

It was about 4::00 am when arriving in Honolulu. I was not tired picked up my luggage and asked myself what do I do now and where would I go? God impressed me to get on the first city bus. I Did! The bus went all the way to Ala Moana. "Last stop" the bus driver said. When I got off there was a park bench on which I sat. Being wide awake on eastern daylight time (about noon) I just sat.

As I sat there, I looked down the street and noticed a YMCA and thought, *I know the Philadelphia YMCA had rooms maybe this one had rooms.*

There was a clerk behind the counter, I asked if there were any rooms available, if not could I reserve one. He said that they do not take reservations and that it was first come first serve. I sat in the lobby a while to watch local news. Moments later A man rushed down the stairs needing to check out. As the man was checking out the clerk said I could have his room and that I had to pay in advance for each day I stayed. I paid in advance and stayed there for about three weeks.

During the days I would walk Ala Moana Park and the mall across the street. Sometimes watch TV in the YMCA lobby.

While staying at the YMCA, I made a list of everyone I knew so I could pray for them individually. When I started it was about noon, but when I finished it was dark outside and went to bed sleeping soundly.

The first Sunday I found a Southern Baptist church in Waikiki. Waikiki Baptist Church would be my home church while Dr. Herman Ray was pastor there, the next few years until he retired.

I went early in order to experience the Sunday school. The singles class met out on the lanai (porch) of the church. This wonderful group of singles embraced me like family. I had not felt so welcomed and instantly accepted in all my life, including other churches I had been in. This certainly was not like the typical churches in the Bible belt.

The whole time in that class, that day I was telling them my story and the situation that I was in. It was like they were glued to every word. I had even shared about my experience with the Holy Spirit.

Lydia Smith was our Sunday school teacher along with her husband George. Lydia was also the secretary of the church. She mentioned that I should go to the Veterans office and get some help there about getting a job. Veterans had priority in those days especially in Hawaii.

That afternoon after church, I walked by the apartment where my wife had stayed, I had been told she was traveling with her new boyfriend a well to do businessman. As I got close, I noticed in the parking lot was my car. It was in my name and, and I had the keys! I got in started it up and drove away.

Was God supplying all my needs, yes! *(Philip. 4:19)*

Now if I landed a job, I would have transportation.

The next day I went to the Veterans' administration office where I filled out several forms. I was told there was a job at an oil refinery, that my experience with pumps, pipes and lab work from the water department in Florida might be something they were looking for. The veteran's office set up and appointment for me the next day.

It was Tuesday I had my interview and was hired. Interesting fact that the person that interviewed me was a man I was stationed with in Korea. There is a saying in Hawaii about getting good jobs (it is not what you know that will get you hired, it is who you know) I started work the very next day. It did not take long for me to get the hang of things and the pay was good.

I needed to establish a permanent address. I found and apartment close to the beach and close to the church in Waikiki.

It was nice, hanging out with the singles class during the times not working shift. Our activities as a group were working the hotel services that Waikiki Baptist conducted, and there was a bunch of them, sixteen in all at that time all up and down Waikiki. On some occasions we would attend the Waikiki Beach Resort chaplaincy that had services on the beach at the Hawaiian Hilton Hotel.

Close to the church was a Christian club that was sponsored by Teen Challenge located on Fort De Russey. On weekends that place was packed, many times Christian celebrities would come by and perform and or preach. Groups from the

U.S. mainland would come to share. It was the place to be on Friday and Saturday evenings for the Christian.

Life was good, really good however, the one thought I could not let go of was my daughter, where was she, and when would I get to see her. She was my family even though small, just the two of us.

When I had been in Hawaii before I looked like a typical haole (white guy in Hawaiian). There would be one special person in our Sunday school group that would help me to adapt to Hawaiian culture, Cliff K. Cliff a pure Hawaiian.

While a student at a local university, Cliff worked as a janitor at the church and other places. He had a lot of spare time and spent it with me teaching, always teaching. He would laugh at me trying Hawaiian words with my deep southern accent.

He taught me that there were multiple ethnic and cultural groups. Although living in the islands, these groups maintained their cultural identity. Each culture had their own way of doing things and different reactions to many things. Cliff told me I had to be familiar with the dos and don'ts when around them.

He took me to a church that was all Hawaiian. Practicing what he had taught me, I was embraced by these wonderful people and was surprised that Hawaiian food, in taste was similar to southern food.

The best part was, that Cliff took me to surfing places where tourists were not likely to go. Cliff even told me how I should dress to stop looking like tourist.

Surprised, Cliff informed me of his experience with the Holy Spirit, he noted that several at Waikiki Baptist had the experienced it including praying in tongues. Even the pastor, Dr. Ray was opened to the members experiences with the Holy Spirit.

It did not take long, a few in the church told me that Cliff had a problem, he was bisexual. He had a girlfriend, Mary, they were always together when Cliff was not working. The time knowing Cliff, he never indicated an interest in men to me.

That did not bother me except for the fact there were some assumed that I was gay because Cliff and I hung out together so much. Not so, Cliff was my personal guide to Hawaiian life and lifestyle and he was a surfer and a fantastic good friend.

My wife of 47 years knows that I am not gay nor have ever been. I learned early being rejected by family how it felt to be rejected. I was never going to reject anyone even if they were gay, rich or poor, sinner or saint, red and yellow black and white – all are precious in His site. After all the only people Jesus rejected was the hypocritical religious leaders that gave him a pain in his behind. Christ had his focus on those that needed him, wanted him, and trusted in him.

Most of all, Cliff was deep spiritually, the songs he wrote and sang were like coming from angels. Many years later after going to Bible college and seminary, coming back to Hawaii, I was eager to find Cliff when my family and I returned

I found out that Cliff had died and gone to be with Jesus. I will see him again someday. What he taught me helped me to survive. "Hang around more with locals than with white folks, you will learn more." He would tell me.

My wife and I had the honor of meeting his wife and children. I had told her how Cliff had helped me, making me into a *kamaaina.* (Regular local type guy)

A Calling – Can't Be Me – a Big Miracle

On off days, I would spend my time working the Hotel services. Before long, I was leading the singing and being the MC of the services, I worked at. I had learned to be bold working with Dr. Ray. He was so open talking to anybody anytime without hesitation.

One day a member of the church came to me and said," Rick, I think God has a call on your life." I responded, "I don't think so, I am soon to be a divorced man." Then she responded, "Don't limit God, Rick, he can open doors for you." That was Sue Nishikawa. The Hawaii Baptist Convention named the state missions offering after Sue.

Later another part time speaker at the church and hotels was retired police Chief and wonderful friend, Dan Liu mentioned he thought I would do good in full time ministry.

Sue was right. It brought back memories of something that happened when I was a child about 10 years old.

I had done something very bad when I was a young boy back in Cartersville, Ga. Mom said that when dad comes home, I am in for it. A good whipping meant dad was going to use his belt on my buttocks and my back. When mom gave me, a whipping it was always with a hickory switch on the legs on my ankles. The belt would always make large red marks on my body, taking weeks to heal. I think today that would be called abusive.

I ran into a cotton field across the road about sunset hiding and praying. I remember telling God, *save me from this*, I would do anything, even if I had to be a preacher or missionary to Africa. just save me from what was coming.

Well, dad had meetings. It was bedtime for me, and mom totally forgot it. That had haunted me, years. Time again and again well into adulthood I would remember what I promised God. It was going to be payback time. I would keep my promise to God by giving my life to serve Him.

A Wednesday night after mid-week services, I went home to my apartment and prayed. Once again, I bargained with God. I said this, "If when my daughter comes to the age of accountability that she would come to Christ, I will go any-where to do anything, anytime, that I will serve you what-ever you want me to do, even if I never see her again on this earth, I will see her with you." I cried myself to sleep that night thinking I would never see her on this earth again.

I went to work and continued to do what I normally do. It was late on the next Wednesday night when I came back to my apartment in Waikiki about 11:30 pm I saw a note wedged in my door with a note with an address and phone number the note said: "Please come quickly and pick up your daughter any-time." I drove to the address. It was where another one of my wife's friends lived. I picked up my daughter, Stephanie, along with a bag of clothes and such.

My wife's lawyer was in contact with me, I went in to his office and signed what is the equivalent to a no-fault divorce. It would be a clean break giving me full custody of my daughter, plus she had given up any visitation rights. I signed the papers it was done. We were now a family of two. My life was now, a working single parent. Lord help me because I was going to need it. How will I take care of my daughter working shift work? I did get help, especially two wonderful girls that were in my church at that time. Eve and Phyllis. I thank God for these ladies. I pray that God would richly reward them.

I had moved to an apartment closer to work. It would be a little easier. I know that as a single parent it is extremely difficult to work my scheduling.

In my mind, I decided to start dating with the prospects of finding a wife. Otherwise, a sure return to life in Florida was inevitable. Proverbs 18:22 came to mind.

Waking to a strange sound; walking in the kitchen to find the garbage disposal had been turned on in my apartment. Running in the kitchen my daughter about to put a spoon in the disposal. I ran and turned it off. I was shaking with fear of what could have happened. I had to do something.

I was off that day and started to pray and seek God for answers. My lifestyle had put a burden on my friends who were trying to help me. "What am I to do Lord?" was my big question.

God always gives answers, if we tune in to Him and listen. My answer was to call my parents to come and take my daughter with them for a while until I could find out what God wanted me to do stay in Hawaii or return to Florida. At that time, they were retired living in a much smaller home.

That was a sad day to see my daughter leave with my parents flying back to Florida. "Oh God, what am I supposed to do"

My goal was to have a family due to the fact that I never felt a part of the family I grew up with. It was tough letting my daughter go. I knew that was the right decision at the time.

I went as far as to do some dating, that led to dead ends. I gave up with the thought that if God wanted me to marry, he would take care of things and give me a sign. I was on the verge of moving back to Florida and making plans. I knew that I could get good work there. God had other plans; I didn't see it until it came, so suddenly.

It was difficult but funny in a way, all my friends at church would joke, "watch out now, Rick is looking for a wife." Now I am on the verge of going back to Florida those voices became silent. One day, before church, it was a habit for all the gang to go across the street to a local café for coffee.

I was at the point of giving up after dating. I was asked, "Do you think you will ever get married "All of them knew I was about to go back to Florida. Responded jokingly, "If God wants me to marry, she will have to come up to me and kiss me right on the cheek!"

The joking had died down that day, until a newly hired waitress came up and kissed me on the cheek saying, "Happy Easter." It was Easter on April the 4th 1974. The gang laughed making sounds of ooooh and aaaah. But on Sunday August the 4th of that year, I married that girl and as I write, we have been married for 47 years as of this book.

We dated and it seemed like everything clicked. I had not felt such love ever. I had been burned so many times, yet with her I was willing to take the risk.

One evening we had met a Spirit filled woman from Texas that attended the evening service at Waikiki Baptist. This lady was full of God's spirit and told me that if I had the faith to marry her, God would show me she was the one he had for me all along. In my mind, how did she even know my situation? – That was God.

The Small Planned Wedding Grew to a Big One

We decided to have a small wedding right after the morning worship at Waikiki Baptist Church. With a few friends. The

Sunday morning of the wedding, arriving early at the church when Dr. Ray, the pastor came running up to me.

"Rick, you have to see this!" He opened the door to the sanctuary, the church was entirely decorated for a wedding: flowers, candelabras, a white train in the middle isle, it had everything. "Dr Ray, I can't afford this."

Dr Ray told me the day before he conducted a large wedding for a couple from Japan. (Dr Ray spoke fluent Japanese) they told Dr. ray to keep all the decorations they had bought for the church to use.

Then, more shocking information, my bride's mother had catered to wedding to feed 300. That was more food than we planned for guest. We decided to invite all the tourist that attended the morning worship to stay for a Hawaiian style wedding. (They did)

There were church members at that time that were professional Hawaiian entertainers that brought their band and hula girls to perform. It was glorious, it was God!

A week after we married, I found out that we lived a couple of blocks from each other in Korea. Her dad was in the Marines. She frequently visited a missionary's house that worked with Christian GIs stationed in Korea. I was invited to go there several times, but wanted to drink and gamble at the club... boy I could have saved myself a lot of pain if I had started going there. The Texas woman was right, she was always the one for me.

Sometimes, we have to make many mistakes in order for us to depend on God for directions. It is a learning process. We grow into obedience. I am grateful for what God has done, putting us together. Was it a perfect marriage? No, we had all the trials, arguments and plenty of disagreements, yet we survived.

Onetime a lady asked, if God had the right girl for you why did you have a baby with your first wife? I answered, God knows the reason, talk to him. Truth is that if I did not have her, I would never have left Florida. God wanted me to be in Hawaii.

God put us together! A short time after we married, we flew to Melbourne to visit my parents introducing my wife. Kathy. Dad took me aside and said," Rick, that girl really loves you I can see it!"

From the moment my daughter saw Kathy, she shouted *Mommy, that is my new mommy*. I believe with all of my heart; God had given me the right person to be my mate.

In time my family would grow. My second child would be born, Lani. She was the image of beauty mixed with a quite nature of being an animal lover. Later, my son, Ricky would be born. the athlete of the family.

Besides the kids we had, we have had many people live with us for periods of time over the years… we took the stranger in and helped them and still do from time to time. One time, I counted we had over 80 people live with us for short periods of time over the years.

The longest was a girl from the Marshall Islands she lived with us for over three years.

New Wife – New Life – No More Shift Work – Bible Studies

Like all marriages there are adjustments. Kathy took right up to my daughter and my daughter to her. We had moved to a couple of locations. Before long, the second daughter, Lani, came along.

We continued to do ministry with the hotels with Dr. Ray. When Dr. Ray retired as pastor of Waikiki Baptist church. A new ministry was launched in our home, the "Aloha Chapel Ministries". Independent from the church where Dr. Ray retired from.

At that time, I did not realize that our biggest ministry would be in our neighborhood, located in Aiea, with the kids that were in high school and college.

We started doing a Bible study in our neighborhood with the local teens and some college students on Sunday after-noons. I went so far as to purchase an autoharp so we could sing the praise songs of the day. I enjoyed watching those kids grow into adulthood. Many miracles happened while we were there.

At work, I was moved to a special duty that got me off shift work, but also provided opportunities to get some extra hours. It was during this time our third child would be born Ricky. He looked so much like my father when I saw him, I said, all he needs is a cigar and he would be the spitting image of my dad. I now had a son, During the next year many radical changes would happen as God began to work in my life, leading me towards full time ministry.

Special Visitors

Not long after we settled in house in Aiea, we were blessed to have three visitors to visit us, my sister, cousin Jan and her son Mark. It was exciting to have family. I took vacation time showing them the island and beaches.

I could see when I took them to one of our hotel's services, they were in shock that I was leading the worship and was the

MC of the service. I don't remember speaking that day but I think I destroyed the image of that young rebellious lad they grew up with.

A year later, my parents came to visit. They did not attend one of our services, but we had a nice visit.

One afternoon Dad and I took a drive up on a hill to view the southside of Oahu, we talked some. Dad said he was surprised at how well I had made a life for myself in Hawaii. I think by that time, both of us had to wipe the tears before we went back to my home. I knew from that moment there was peace between my father and me.

Battles Begin – Who is My Enemy?
Ephesians 6:12

The first time we experienced a direct attack from the forces of evil. That happened when I purchased a Time magazine with an article on how witchcraft was growing in Europe.

Reading the article, finding many items of interest, like most people involved in modern-day witchcraft had started by reading their astrology charts in local newspapers. My interest was the fact that I had friends and family in the that were deep into astrology. I knew astrology was not of God. A relative once told me, "The wise men that came from the East were astrologist." I responded; "yea, they went straight to King Herod – then they had to look in scripture. It was the Word that led them to the Christ Child. "

I had placed the magazine on a shelf, when on one evening my wife had awaken with shadow like demons attacking her. She laughed at them and that made them vanish. Demons try, but cannot overcome the believer in Christ, the fact is that we have power over evil. *James 4: 7*

That day I had discovered that in that magazine there were many symbols of the occult. I burned the magazine. My biggest battle was yet to come.

My next-door neighbor, a senior in a local high school close by came over to ask me if I could speak to her psychology class, that they were studying para psychology. I agreed stating I would work out a schedule at work. The topic she wanted me to speak was prophecy.

That week it seemed as though all hell broke loose in our lives with all kinds of things happening to us including a car accident. I was angry, but I knew where it was coming from. We were under attack from the enemy. To me that would always mean something fantastic was about to happen.

I was to speak that Friday at the school. Getting off work early, I drove a rental car while our car was being fixed. Several miles from our home the car had a flat on the freeway. Looking for a spare tire and jack, there was none.

I began to pray in the spirit, when I stuck out my thumb to hitch a ride. Just seconds after I stuck my thumb out, a young man stopped and drove me directly to our home where I jumped in my VW van and drove to the school just in time, not a minute to spare.

The teacher of the class met me in the school office. She asked me if I could handle the class until school was out because she had a meeting. "Of course." I knew several of the kids in that class, some had attended my Sunday Bible study group.

As I walked into the psychology classroom of a public school, I was horrified. All the walls in the classroom were covered with posters and signs: How to read tarot cards – how to read palms – knowing your astrology signs – and in the class were a couple of we Ouija boards. I was in the devil's playground where young minds are formed. I was going to fight with the most powerful weapon, the word of God, the Bible.

I had prepared that week to present how the Old Testament of the Bible prophesied the coming of Christ and how the prophecy was fulfilled in the New Testament.

To God be the glory, many lives in that classroom were touched and changed. We had overcome by the word of God. God moved in that classroom. From that experience, I began to ponder the thought of going full time into the ministry. God opened that door; the teacher was out for almost two hours in which I talked about Christ in a public school. I felt like I could have made an alter call that day.

The teacher came in a few minutes before the bell rang to dismiss the class asking how it went, thinking the topic of prophecy was more like things you would fine in a cheap tabloid.

Many Christian friends thought I should start a church on my own. I began to seek what God wanted me to do. I had shared this with one of the volunteers with the new ministry, retired police chief Dan Liu, he gave me encouraging words verifying I had a call on my life and that I should consider some form of education in the field of ministry.

Listening to a Christian radio station one day, I heard a statement: (God cannot steer a parked car) I was waiting for God to do something; after listening about not moving, moving by for me started by doing homework, what it would take to be a full-time minister, and the education needed to minister effectively.

Looking at Peter; Peter was an illiterate fisherman. He stayed in Jerusalem most of the time, took a trip to Rome and was crucified upside down.

Paul, however, was well educated probably spoke 3 or more languages (Hebrew, Latin, Greek, and perhaps more) Paul along with his companions that traveled with him, evangelized the Roman world.

The conclusion, was to get a proper education and that would mean a move back to the mainland.

I don't condemn those that choose different paths because that is between them and God. Choosing to get educated was the path and I needed it. I wanted to help people grow in Jesus. I wanted to lead as many as possible to Christ and see them grow. That was going to take a proper education with the help of God

"An investment in knowledge pays the best interest." –
Benjamin Franklin
2 Timothy 2:15

Selling my stock in the company I worked at had tripled the day I sold it, given a substantial resource for the move. It would also be enough to see us through the first year of college.

Time to Say Goodbye – Miracles Happened

I have attended many Christian churches of different denominations quite a few denominations as well as meetings with the Full Gospel Businessmen's' meeting. One thing that would happen on some occasions was something called being *slain in the Spirit of God*. I was very skeptical of this event happening, sometimes watching it looked fakey, people looking back before they fell to make sure someone caught them.

Before we headed to the mainland, we had our Bible study group come over for a fellowship the last time. That evening, it was all girls. The girls had bought me a special gift. A book filled with pictures of paintings of the Life of Jesus, painted by a Jewish man.

The book was, "He was One of Us" by Rein Poortvliet. Publisher – Doubleday. As I thumbed through the book, I was stunned by one of Rein's paintings. It was the face of Christ, while being crucified. It was the same image I saw many years prior while I was sitting on a bunk in that jail cell. That was a powerful confirmation I was on the right track with God.

The night was not over, we all gathered in a circle holding hands. I started to pray our farewell prayer, a few moments later a strange thing happened to us that I did not expect. The presence of holiness filled the room to where the air felt heavy and thick. All of a sudden, we heard the thump and plump of those there with us.

My wife and I opened our eyes to see that all but myself and my wife had been slain in the spirit. After a few moments they all slowly stood up. None of these girls had been in Pentecost or Full Gospel type churches. They were all shocked like we were as we were too. The power of God filled that room.

Some Christians would call this event evil, even Satanic. I know deep in my heart and soul, there was nothing evil about it that evening. Remember those that know Christ have his divine protection.

Let us looks at this event:
1. The term *slain in the spirit* is a modern term.

2. There is no biblical reference to Satan having that kind of power over the children of God.
3. The Bible does not use the term *slain* however there are Biblical events that indicate similar experiences, but not the term of being slain. Acts 9:3-4 - Acts 9:1-43 - Revelation 1:17 - John 18:6 - Matthew 17:6 - Ezekiel 1:28 - 2 Chronicles 5:14 –
4. The problem rest in the battle of those that experience manifestation of the Spirit and those that believe it was only for the early church and not for today's churches.
5. There are those that would also counterfeit this phenomenon and those like us that night that knew it was real.

Another Miracle

The next day, the day before we were to leave for San Francisco, Our dear friend Eve invited my wife and I to dinner. She and Phyllis had done so much for me and my daughter, Stephanie.

When we arrived at Eve's home, she was sad and shared with us that her and her husband were trying to have children, but due to health reasons with Eve, she could not conceive, I was told she had no eggs. I asked," Can we pray for you and anoint you with oil?" She agreed. The only oil we could find was cooking oil. I quoted scripture in the book of James, specifically chapter 5: 14 - 15

I told her that since I am the oldest there, that would make me the elder. Months later after arriving in Florida, Eve mailed us a card telling us she was pregnant. That was God!

The Spiritual Pilgrimage – To Learn and Grow

It is time to move, God can't steer a parked car. I bought a Toyota long bed truck with a small camper shell and had it shipped to San Francisco during the summer of 1979.

Upon arrival, we picked up the truck and I drove the family south to a place in California where my wife knew former missionaries that worked in Korea were operating a Christian camp. We spent a couple of weeks helping them in a most beautiful setting that was bursting with all types of wildlife. Due to the elevation of the camp, it was cold at night and hot/dry during the day.

We set out to our next stop would in Kansas where my wife's uncle and family lived. While we were there, we encountered a hail storm that had damaged the camper shell.

With quick repairs we headed south through Oklahoma and Texas. Late one afternoon in Texas, just north of Houston, at a rest stop on the intrastate highway. I heard two men talking about a hurricane that was about to hit between the coastlines of Louisiana and Mississippi.

I usually do not listen to the radio while driving. I was driving right into a hurricane. I immediately tuned on a radio station that would keep me informed.

We had just driven over the border into Louisiana, when I pulled into a rest stop that appeared to be on high ground. The wind was picking up. The decision was not to drive further. Of course, we prayed for God's protection, we had our two small girls and my infant son.

I felt so ignorant for not being informed, that was a lesson learned when traveling. We slept through the night, the sound of wind and rain outside somehow made us sleep soundly, God brought us through safely.

From there we made a beeline to Melbourne Florida where mom and dad were living since, they retired.

Mom and dad had retired and built a small two bedroom, two bath home. They also had an airstream trailer. They knew we were coming to the mainland in order for me to enroll in a Christian college, but they did not expect us to drive up one afternoon, walk right in the house. Surprise!

One day, they watched the kids while we drove to the college to apply. Southeastern college is located by Lake Bonny in Lakeland, Florida. At that time, it was the only fully accredited Christian college in Florida. Today, Southeastern is a full university and has expanded greatly.

Upon arrival I went to the register's office to apply for the Fall semester. Great news, all my former college credits transferred as well as physical education was accredited with my military experience. The first two years I would use my GI Bill. The great news...I would not have to take any math in order to graduate. Math had always been a major weakness only basic math was what I learned and thank God for hand held calculators.

Shortly after registration, I located an apartment just a few blocks from the college. In a short time, we furnished the apartment going to garage sales, thrift shops and flea markets.

Soon after settling in, we found a Baptist church to attend. Soon, my wife and I were working with the youth until the pastor resigned. The deacons came by that very afternoon to asked me to pastor. Overnight, I had become a Baptist pastor. Before that happened, the church had already licensed and ordained me.

That experience was a hands-on fly by the seat of your pants adventure. Several of my professors not only helped me out, but came often to speak. Truly it was learning by doing. Gratitude goes out to those professors and to students at the school.

Two of the students at the college asked if the church would let them use a small space for an office for the local chapter of Youth for Christ. The church had the perfect small office set up. Later their officials asked If I would serve on the board of the Central Florida division. The crazy part of that I would have to attend and oversee local chapters when they met with high schoolers.

One spring break over 100 students went to a camp in central Florida. I was designated the chief cook supervising having about 8 students to help me prepare breakfast and dinner.

One morning one of the students made cool aid in a 10-gallon pot, then pouring it into 5-gallon containers. I had 4 students to crack eggs to make a massive amount to feed the students and supervisors. Not realizing they used the same container the cool aid had been in. The chemical reaction turned the scrambled eggs green creating an authentic green eggs and ham breakfast.

At that time the church did not have a constitution and bylaws and within the community the church had owed a lot of money that past pastors had ran up large bills that had not been paid. With much work and faith. We had a new constitution and bylaws and all the church's depts were paid off including the outstanding bonds that the church had.

My first funeral that conducted was almost a total disaster. The husband of a church member had died in a hospital. I had visited him at times in the Veteran's hospital in Tampa.

The chapel in the funeral home was new and had a see-through Plexiglass podium. Noticing my wife was pointed to me, as I looked down to see my fly was not only opened but off the zipper's track. I did the whole message holding my notebook low over my lap.

The disaster was not over. At the burial site had a drizzling rainfall. All there squeezed close under a canopy. Facing the head of the casket, I did not realize an honor guard was directly in back of me. After taps was played the honor guard fired the first volley when one of the ejected hot shells landed in my neck collar causing me to turn fast falling partially in the grave. My wife and a gentleman helped me out.

My first baptism at the church was even worse. A deacon had filled the baptistry up to about five inched from the top. The lady I was to baptize was quite large. (I think that she was just over 275 lbs. or more) I was heavy as well weighing about 225lbs. That's 500 lbs. The lady fell from the second step, I jumped in to help her creating a massive tidal wave in the choir loft. (It was a mess but a powerful lesson – mass can and always displaces water).

My wife and I needed to work to add to our dwindling finances – My wife got a job at the college cafeteria. Of course, I had the church and a few odd jobs. We decided to buy a house under the GI Bill. That was affordable. Soon after, with help from my mother-in-law, we moved into a new home while renting the older home to provide the needed extra income.

Because our new home was just across the lake from the collage, and only three blocks to walk, our home became a hangout for students from the college. It was also a place for holidays for those students that were not able to travel home.

Sometimes, we had a bunch of them, that was fun, even our kids enjoyed them.

One year during thanksgiving we had several students to come over. My parents called and said they were coming and bringing special guest. The guest that gave me the greatest thrill that Thanksgiving, was when Coreen and Bill from Cartersville visited with my parents. Coreen and been the catalyst that started my spiritual pilgrimage when I was very young.

The years we were in Lakeland, we took in a lot of students. For us, and I hope for them it was a wonderful experience.

Graduation and Wonderful Words

After many years of neglect and recognition from my parents, my day of graduating from Southeastern College had finally come.

My parents came not only for graduation but stayed for Sunday services at the church I was pastoring. Finally, the words for the first time ever coming from my parents; "We are so proud of you son." It took over 30 years to hear that from the both of them, especially dad. I was so choked up, I wept long and hard that evening in the quietness of our home. This day was long in coming. For the first time I felt special by my parents.

Resignation and Job Hunting – What a Struggle

It saddened my heart to resign the first church that I pastored. I loved the folks there but a problem ensued when a couple I had friended that were students at the college visited our church, they were from Jamaica. At the end of the service three church leaders came to me and told me not to invite *their kind* to our church. I asked why, and they said they have their way of worship and we have ours. The real problem was the fact that they were black.

I resigned. It is interesting that my wife is Asian and several times I had a fine distinguished black man from the Bahamas come and speak. (Asa Butler – his father was the first elected governor of the Bahamas) We also had a lady from Korea she had been retired from being the secretary of Yongi Cho's church in Korea. Too often prejudice pops up to surprise you.

From that point, I began to send out resumes and continued daily to check the bulletin board at the college for jobs that were listed.

Finally, there was a job that looked good a Christian school in California was looking for a school chaplain. I rushed a letter of interest to them and a response came quickly wanting a personal interview with me as soon as I could make it.

It was late March that year that I drove across the USA to California for an interview that lasted only a few minutes. The job listing was for a Chaplain to conduct devotions and counsel students. When I got there the job description had totally changed and they were not interested in me. Actually, the school had obtained a new dean.

Walking out. I asked God, *Why me?* I felt like I wasted my time and money, which at that time money was not much to work with.

While heading back over the mountains, a late spring snow storm developed blocking several passages over the Sierra Nevada Mountains. Therefore, I kept heading southward to find a passage that was open using up a lot of gas and time, money was getting low.

I was tired with very little sleep when I wound up in Bishop California. I got a room just outside the town, rooms were expensive because the mountains had snow for the skiers and it was the opening of trout season for fishermen. I had to get some sleep.

Tired and my old nemesis, anger once again began to well up in me. I was angry at God. "Why did you bring me all this way for nothing?"

That morning I asked the manager what is the fastest way to go eastward over these mountains I needed to get to Las Vegas as soon as possible. He gave instructions to use a small maintenance road and that it would be well over a hundred miles before I would see any sign of civilization. I needed to gas up and carry extra water.

I followed his advice. After filling up with gas and buying bottled water, I only had 12 dollars left. I would drive to Las Vegas and get help from a friend that worked there.

A few miles up the maintenance road, I spotted a hitch hiker standing in some snow. Stopping to pick him up, the good Christian thing to do. Introducing myself as Pastor Rick, he said his name was John and that he had just got out of prison and was headed home.

In my mind thinking, "Okay God, is this going to be my end, robbed and left in the wilds to die!" My train of thought broke when he spoke, "Don't worry Rev. While in prison, I got saved. (What a relief).

He told me that when we get on the Nevada side of the mountain, the road splits – North to Reno where his mom was and South to Las Vegas where I was going.

We had great fellowship, even singing some praise songs. I knew this meeting was meant for the both of us. It had given me reassurance that God was guiding me which I really needed at that time.

John was thinking about going to a Christian college to become a chaplain. Was it God, that he was thinking about going to Southeastern! I told John all about Southeastern.

I shared with him of my struggles of finding where God wanted me. Without telling him of my situation he said. "Why don't you consider going to seminary for your graduate degree?"

"John, I said, that is what I am going to do."

It was about 1PM when we came to the fork in the road. I noticed there was nothing, no shade, no plants, no water. I asked him, *How for up the road before you came to some kind of civilization.* He told me about 40 miles. He told me not to worry that usually about sunset there would be some traffic going north.

That would be 80 miles out of my way. If God linked us up, I could not let him out there. I drove him up the road, let him in out in a small farming community and then I headed for Las Vegas. He wanted to give me some money to pay for gas. I told him, "Don't worry the Lord will provide." I was planning on meeting a friend in Vegas that could loan me some money.

I don't know what ever happened to John, but I know he is in God's hand.

My friend was the chaplain of the Las Vegas Strip. After meeting him in Hawaii, my wife and I spent time with him while we were on our honeymoon there. All the detours due to the snow, had and drained me down to my last 12 dollars. How was I to make it back, Las Vegas to Florida on 12 dollars?

Years ago, Las Vegas was much smaller and so were most of the casinos. I had been through there twice before and it was easy to find you way around.

In Vegas I went straight to my friend's office located in one of the major casinos, only to find out he was on vacation in Hawaii. His secretary was in a rush to get to her son's little league game.

What now, just 12 dollars to get me back to Florida. I remembered what I told John, that God would provide, thinking if I found a Western Union office, I could have dad wire me enough to get me back home. I could sleep in the parking lot, there were hundreds of cars there thinking I would be safe.

As I walked out, I stopped and asked a waitress where a Western Union office might be. After she told me, I started to walk out when she gave me a token. "What's this for, I asked." "You can't leave without playing, just put it in one of our machines."

I stopped at the first slot machine to put the token in and walked out with over two hundred dollars. (don't get me wrong, I am not a gambler other that family fun, very low stakes, Texas hold-em.) I filled the car with gas. I went to a steak house ate dinner (not eaten for the past 2 days,) then I bought small souvenir gifts for the wife and kids.

It was dark when I went across into Arizona and spent the night at a rest stop. I made my way back to Florida and began making plans to go to a seminary. That would take some time applying and waiting for approval.

Back at home a neighbor approached me about filling in as pastor until they could hire a pastor from their own denomination. I said yes. Before we left Lakeland, that church made my family and I honorary lifetime members and I had steady income. God did that!

I had applied and was accepted at a seminary in California; however, Proper housing for my family was not available. I shared this with dad. He responded, a man in his church knew the dean at Southwestern Baptist Theological Seminary in Fort Worth, Texas.

Later, I was told that since the seminary in California accepted me, I would be able to attend Southwestern Baptist Seminary under that acceptance. They said if I could be there In January, I could start in the spring semester.

We packed up again and moved to Texas. We sold the first home we obtained and rented our newer home as a source on extra income. God had our situation well in control, He wanted me at Southwestern for a good reason, he wanted us back in Hawaii.

Here We Go Again – Life in Texas – The Kids Are Growing.

In a short time, the family settled in to an apartment complex in which my wife landed a job as assistant manager, while I worked doing painting and make-ready and repairs in vacant apartments. The kids were in a school close by; everything was working out ... God did it for us!

On Sundays I conducted worship services in a senior citizen assisted living center that was also located within the apartment complex. It was not long, I was playing games, calling bingo and visiting the tenets.

The kids were enrolled in school close by but my commute was about 30 miles round trip. We found out that Arlington was better for us than living in Fort Worth. Because my wife was the on-site assistant manager, our 3-bedroom apartment was free. God provides for those that seek Him and follow him wherever he leads.

The first semester I was enrolled in a Master of Divinity degree. I was getting the same teaching as I got at Southeastern College. Later, I found out that most all of the Bible professors in college, had earned their degrees at Southwestern. The class outlines were the same or similar.

I went to administration to discuss this and they recommended I change my program to a master of religious education. I did and it was the best to my advantage. Much of the studies included counseling, church administration and educational techniques with curriculum design. One of my projects I needed to have, was designing an education program for the church I attended.

Soon while I was doing school studies, one of my professors, Dr Caldwell, noticed that I had lived in Hawaii. "Rick, did you know that there is a Hawaii club with several students and their families?" Caldwell was the student advisor of the club. Years after graduation, he would visit Hawaii from time to time visiting myself and others. I would also have three other professors visit me in Hawaii.

I met with the Hawaii club at one of their meetings and it was fantastic. Within a years' time, I was elected vice president. Looking back at that, it forged deep friendships.

I believe our children had an adventure, themselves. The oldest was already in high school, the middle was in intermediate school and the youngest was in elementary school. Our biggest family events were going to the Texas Ranger ball games. It was nice to have relatives close by. My father's sister and family lived in Dallas. On holidays and sometimes just to visit, we would drive over for a visit. We had taken advantage of the many things to do that blossomed into wonderful memories.

Graduation – Immediate Opportunity, Hawaii Here I Come Again

I was notified by one of the Hawaii Baptist convention executives that an immediate opportunity might be able if I was interested. A church on the island of Kauai had been without a pastor for a couple of years. I was told that they needed one ASAP.

My big question, *was this a temporary position*? The answer was that it was but there would be no time limit. I agreed that I would do it, if the church would consider me in view of a call.

Soon after that a retired pastor that lived in Fort Worth called me and wanted to meet with me to talk about the church. Telling me he had been the last interim pastor; he had given me some warning that this particular church was considered the most difficult to pastor because there were no men in leadership positions.

He gave me names of those that would give me support and those that would become a pain in the butt. He had been there a while. He told me the harvest was white because born again Christians were few on that island. In a short time, he was right about those that would be a pain.

Graduation was a very special time for me, it would begin to be a time of total healing between my parents and I. Mom and Dad were driving up from Florida to spend a few days and to attend my graduation. Dad was also eager to visit his sister in Dallas.

I asked my mother if there was something that she would like to do while they were in Texas. She told me that she had always wanted to see a professional sport like football or baseball.

My daughter Stephanie, worked at the Texas Rangers Stadium at that time. We managed to get prime seats behind first base. That night the San Diego Chicken was visiting there to entertain. I know from the expression on mom's face, that she had a great time. I did everything I could to make my parents welcomed and happy. Maybe we could build a new relationship.

My graduation was the next day and my parents were going to spend the night with dad's sister in Dallas, then head back to Florida. In two days, I would be flying back to Hawaii.

Late that night, I saw a light on in the kitchen. I walked in to find mom at the dining table awake eating some cookies. I asked her, "Are you alright mom?" She answered in a strange way. "You have forgiven me, haven't you?" I told her that I did both for her and Dad. We hugged.

That morning, we all got up to see mom and dad leave. At that time, I did not know that mom was in the early stages of Alzheimer's disease, linked with dementia, the years of alcohol and medications had taken a toll on mom. After she and dad left that day, she would never know again who I was.

The next day, I was on a non-stop to Hawaii. I got there early in the morning and took a cab to my mother-in-law's home in Aiea. Kathy's aunt, Jun was so eager to see me, she was banging on the window for me to open the door.

Deep down in my heart, I knew and felt like I was back where I belonged and that God had put me there for his purposes. Late that morning I drove a borrowed car to the Baptist convention office to meet with officials in the office.

I knew all of them from before in the hotel ministry and those that had visited the seminary. In the office was, the director, and a couple of local pastors that I had known.

The first thing they asked me is if I knew anything about the church. I told them of having lunch with the last interim pastor in Texas. He told the church had a bad reputation about how they treated their pastors. Those leaders shared the same thing. One of the officials flew with me over to Kauai to meet with a small group of church leaders.

I stayed half the summer, when one of the older ladies came by the parsonage to give me some advice. She told me If I wanted to stay with the church, the members would want to meet my wife. At that time, they did not know that my wife was Asian. Most all of the members were Asians.

I flew my wife over to meet with the church members. They immediately were impressed by her appearance and her mannerism. I expressed the need to know if they were interested in me as their full-time pastor because my children had to be enrolled in a school somewhere that fall. It was already July.

Though some wanted to wait another year, I gave them the ultimatum that I needed a decision before fall. Shortly after the church voted me as their new pastor with only one negative vote. Strange, but I knew who gave me the negative vote.

I had to go back to Texas to get ready to move. The church was generous to help us financially for the move. Some would call it irony; I call it *GOD!* I fought the idea of going to seminary for over two years while this church was without a pastor for the same length of time.

Things were smooth for a good while. At first the kids were apprehensive about going to a small island. However, in a very short time their attitude rapidly changed. They quickly made new friends.

Eventually, because the parsonage was located next to the church the home become the center of activities, especially for the high school kids. There is not much to do on Kauai. The saying goes, they roll up the sidewalks by 5pm. All of our kids had graduated from high school there moving on to greater things.

In a few short years I had conducted the wedding services for many of those high school kids that were regulars in our home and there were those that I baptized when they became Christians. With memories being shallow in my seventies, my wife told me that I had baptized over three hundred, that of course, I think that included the two other churches I pastored in Hawaii.

During my stay, I had also conducted over 300 weddings including several weddings of celebrities and well know businessmen that had brand name franchises all over the U.S. and Canada. Two of these weddings, guests were flown over from the mainland in private jets with over 200 guest and family members in each. I was blessed to see one of those well know a producer for a large television network came to the Lord in the pre-marital counseling I required.

In order to do ministry on the island more efficiently, I eagerly joined an ecumenical group of clergies from all different Christian denominations. Their friendship and comradery will cling to me for all eternity. I learned quickly that the culture on Kauai was very different from the other islands, things were done differently than the norm.

One day I shared with the group that I found out that I had bleeding ulcers. An older Catholic priest took me aside to talk. "Do you know the sacraments of our church?" I told him I knew. "Your Baptist, I am Catholic would you agree that we would agree on most of the Bible?"

I said," of course."

At that he anointed me with oil and prayed for my healing in Latin. I had an appointment the very next day to get my second endoscope revealing that my stomach was healed. I learned; God can use anyone that embraces Christ as God's son.

A couple of years later during an ecumenical service, I brought the message at his church.

My wife started some part time work with the Salvation Army, the next thing, I was asked to serve on the board for the local Salvation Army by a charismatic Episcopal priest that was on the board. We became good friends playing golf on a regular basis.

From this group, I launched into asking about hospital chaplaincy and was included in the chaplains list. The hospital provided extra training in the form of CPE (clinical pastoral education) Most of us that took the courses achieved four units of CPE.

Becoming familiar with doctors and staff made my job easy. Many of them were Christians. One day a couple of Christian doctors approached me about conducting services early Sunday mornings. When they worked Sunday shifts, they did not have opportunities to worship. The church was only two blocks from the hospital I started early services for them.

That first Sunday we had about 25. Nothing fancy, singing, some prayer and a short message. Before long word had gotten around to some of the hotels; we started getting tourist to attend those services. That way they had more time for activities on the island later in the day.

First Out of the Nest – It Was Hard on Me

My first born had graduated. The policy I laid before my kids, after they graduated, they could spend one year doing what they wanted to do. At the end of the year, they had three choices: got to school full time, get a full-time job, or enlist in the military. Eventually she went into the military. My struggles over time to get her, made it difficult to let her go. She was eighteen years old and an adult.

I had promised my Stephanie when she turned eighteen, I would try to find her biological mother. I knew she was still in Honolulu. With the help of my mother-in-law, I flew her to Honolulu to meet with her. Stephanie had always considered Kathy, my wife to be her only mother, Kathy raised her as her own.

The meeting with the biological mother was short. To my surprise she admitted to our daughter she was the one at fault.

A strange thing happened a couple of weeks later, I had to fly to Honolulu for a meeting. I would always stay with my mother-in-law. Shortly after I arrived, she told me that my former mother-in-law had become a devout Christian and wanted to talk to me. I said fine. She dialed the number only to get my former wife on the phone. Handing me the phone, "Opps, this is your first wife."

I had not spoken to her in over 16 years, what is the world am I going to say? Speaking first, "Listen, this is awkward for the both of us. I want you to know that I have forgiven you and that I am happy with a wonderful family." Immediately she began crying telling me she carried that burden of guilt of what she did to me that gave her such agony she had bleeding ulcers and had to have part of her stomach removed. Then she said, "Today, you have set me free with your forgiveness." That was it, we both hung up our phones. That day I learned how powerful and empowering of what forgiveness can be and do.

Hurricane (Iniki) – Clean Up – Food Prep – Big Headaches

Things were going well, I even served on the advisory council with the mayor's office as well as on a committee with the Hawaii Baptist Convention.

Things were fine until September 11, 1992. A category 4 hurricane, "INIKI" hit the Kauai with sustained wind of 145 MPH with gust up to 225 MPH. There was advance warning however, for hours on end from early morning till the storm hit sirens were constantly blowing. There were only a few hours of daylight to prepare until the storm hit.

I decided the best place for us was in the church sanctuary. The walls of the church were brick tiles and the roof was supported by steel beams.

My oldest daughter had graduated and had listed in the US Army and was stationed in Germany at that time. There was the four of us in my family, also a Japanese student we were housing for a friend, and a contractor and his wife that were staying in the churches garage apartment.

Things were fine for the first 40 minutes or so, wind was increasing. Soon after we heard glass breaking all over. My wife and daughter were sitting on the front pew; as I noticed glass was breaking around the church, I told them to move to the back of the church away from windows. A few short moments after they moved a large beam from somewhere came through the front window and landed on the pew, I had told them to move from. THAT WAS GOD! I know if they had stayed on that bench they would have been seriously injured.

As we all huddled in the back in the restroom area that was all concrete block, we felt safe. Moments after that another giant beam came through the roof of the church creating a massive hole. (Later we measured that beam to be = 8" X 3' X 20 plus feet long. (weeks later it would take about 20 men to pull that beam out,

When it was over, we thanked God. To our amazement other than some shingles and a few broken windows, there was little damage to the parsonage. However, half of the educational building was destroyed. All of us were stressed and tired. With a quietness that seem almost too good to be true, we all slept soundly that evening.

Waking up at daylight while the others were sleeping, I wanted to look at the damage. Every telephone pole was down on our street, most houses of my neighbors were spared with some damage. There was debris everywhere. There was not a single leaf on any tree or bush it was strange looking.

Looking down the street where one of my church members lived. The house was gone only a fraction of a wall was left. I grieved thinking she and her husband had died. (They had stayed in a proper shelter) Thank you Father!

We didn't do much that day other than listen to the radio. On the main road several cars and trucks had flat tires due to all the glass and boards with nails in the street.

Sunday morning, I conducted a simple worship service. Several members and a couple of tourists and a news reporter showed up. We thanked God, sang some and then had a briefing telling those there that help would be on the way. Some stayed a while to help us clean up the sanctuary. However, that was a large task for such a short time, at least the pews were cleaned, later, volunteer workers would sleep on the pews or on the floor in the educational building that was half gone.

That afternoon, I sat in my office which was located in the parsonage. When I heard the sweetest voice from one of the Hawaii Baptist Convention employees," Rick are you home?"

"Yes, how did you get here so soon."

I replied. I was told the Baptist relief, worked with the red cross and he came in with them to survey the needs. He told me he was going to stay with a relative and get back with me. Thank God for Stanley Togigawa.

Next day, he told me that a group was flying in late in the afternoon and that I needed to prepare sleeping quarters for them. I spent the day cleaning up what I could, not knowing how many there would be. Late that afternoon, with the church van we had a group of about twenty-four. A Baptist relief leader from another state came in later that night and immediately conducted a meeting with the volunteers.

I learned that due to hurricane relief from hurricane Andrew, that had hit Florida, most of the Baptist relief teams were in Florida.

Next, he said that our teams on Kauai could only do kitchen food prep, to serve meals to the people on the island. He also said that all workers other that the team that was present, would have to come from our local church members. I spoke up and told the group that most of our members had major damage to their homes and the volunteer pickings was going to be very slim. In time 95 percent of the volunteers that served in the relief effort kitchen would come in from other islands. There was little damage from the other islands, Kauai had it bad.

The next thing that happened was a horrible mistake. The governor of Hawaii decided that since all the schools on Kauai had very little damage, that the schools would start up immediately. My wife worked at the high school and my two kids were students there. While school was on, I would be alone on the premises of the church. Other churches and pastors in the community would have the same or similar problems.

The Baptist volunteers set up a large kitchen and dining area in a local auditorium. Food was served there and brought to other locations on the island.

Due to the damage, at the church, doors were damaged providing opportunities for looters to rummage through the personal items of the volunteers and inside the other buildings. I actually got chewed out by one of the volunteers for leaving their items unguarded. Remember, I am alone on the premises.

I ran a few of the looters away with my son's baseball bat. All I had to do is threaten them by hitting their vehicles with the bat... they left peacefully.

Because the church was centralized within the community it became a gathering/meeting place for all the volunteer organizations in order to coordinate their work. It was necessary to keep as many people on the premises during the day as possible.

There, at those meetings in the church, information was shared that the local pastors in our group were going through the same thing – big demands from the volunteers and church members with little help with the church facilities that we had to stand guard. We were promised that the Law would help us by watching the facilities. But they were stretched thin too.

As ministers, all of us were at our wit's end with demands placed on us from church members, volunteer workers, and the hospital. But all of us were alone, everyone was bushed, it was difficult for us to leave the churches unattended, but we all were called to help outside the church.

As more volunteers came. Ladies were coming as well. We were asked to allow the ladies to sleep in the parsonage. From time to time, we had from eight to twelve ladies sleep on the living room floor. That meant little time in our home for our own bathroom times and washing and bathing our bodies. We still had my kids, the exchange student. (Only two bathrooms for fifteen to twenty people)

There was an Army Officer that came to the parsonage one day. He had been told that we had a solar hot water heater. He asked me if he could bath each day in the early afternoons and that he had a specific skin condition. I told him that was fine, it was nice to have someone on the premises besides me. After a couple of days, he asked me if there was something he could do for me. I told him if he could secure some cots that would make our volunteers more comfortable than on the floor or church pews.

The next day an Army truck drove up, behind that another truck full of soldiers. They unloaded 100 cots. Then, the soldiers cleaned up all the debris around the church and par-sonage. Wow, that officer could come and bath any time he wanted to! I would even scrub his back.

Pastors needed to meet with each other to discuss our needs and problems we were having, sharing how we could handle them. At times meeting sometimes the minister's including myself would breakdown and cry. Would you even dare to think all of us pastors had complaints coming in that we were not doing enough? Here are some of the things I heard while being totally alone during daylight hours along with the other pastors as other pastor had the same kind:

Pastor – why aren't you down at the kitchen helping us?

Pastor – what are you doing at the kitchen go back and watch the church

We are shorthanded at the hospital we need you now our staff is dangerously short, chaplain please!

Pastor -Who is watching the generator pastor get a chain and lock to secure it – (later after I secured a chain and lock, I had to run some thieves off with the baseball bat and calling the police giving a description of their truck?)

Pastor - There is water where we are sleeping, why didn't you mop it up we are tired, what have you been doing all day?

Pastor - When are you coming to our house to help us clean up and bring the chainsaw – (at times I did chain saw visitation to church members and neighbors)?

Pastor - Don't forget you have to pick up and drop off volunteers at the airport.

Hey pastor, there is a drug store just opened, can you get my subscription filled for me?

Keep in mind we are still doing services on Sundays and chaplain duties at the hospital were critical due to the fact staff had to take care of their own homes and many of the staff left the island.

One day about mid-morning all alone, I sat out on the stoop of the educational building, when one of the volunteers came back to the church to retrieve something he had forgotten to take with him. He noticed I was sitting on the stoop in anguish.

I was startled when he came upon me telling me, "It's alright pastor, I have been to many of these all over the USA." As soon as he put his arm around me, I lost control with my emotions. After a few moments, he lit up a cigar giving me one. We just sat there a good while. It was the first time I felt compassion in a time of great need.

Pastors like myself were accused of hiding or being lazy. However, the churches on the west side of the island, all the efforts for recovery were right there at their church, they did not have to do anything but stay at their church helping their own community with a mass of volunteers to accommodate them on the premises. While on our side of the island, all were spread out.

A big surprise happened one day. A large truck dropped off a shipping container. I had to sign the release. I was told another church had some items in the container. Noticing who sent the container sent me waves of joy. It was the 700 Club, Operation Blessing. Opening the container it had tarps, cases of diapers among other items of need. The truck driver said I had only 24 hours to unload the container. The rest of the day was spent well into the evening unloading the container by myself. The last items were cases of Bibles. I was exhausted doing that, but was confronted by a volunteer from another island, "Why aren't you doing anything pastor your just stay here most all of the time doing nothing."

Before Christmas, I noticed that fewer people came in and those that did were contractors that were looking for a free meal. Some tried to sneak in and pass themselves off as volunteers to sleep in the church facilities. I kicked many of them and so did the other pastors out with the help of the law. They could pay for rooms in a hotel and boost the economy after all they were making profit from our misery.

Moving on now, the recovery was exhausting for pastors and their families. Every week or two picking up volunteers at the airport usually 8 to 12 at a time. They would stay a week or two then go back while another group came in. Very little rest for pastors and their families. The volunteers were fresh and rested when they arrived, while we who lived it from day to day had little rest and yet many volunteers had become more of a pain than help. Here is how I would classify volunteers:

The quiet compassionate volunteers with understanding of what we were going through day by day. Helping in anyway needed.

The bossy volunteers (been to other disasters) they don't do anything but tell everybody what they need to be doing.

The take me on a tour volunteer – all they want to do is drive around site seeing taking photos

The stand arounders – they just stand around talking but not working, but they were there.

The complainers – they complain about everything but do nothing to solve their own problems.

Many pastors and church members had moved off island by Christmas; which had put a greater pressure on the pastors and staffs that stayed.

It took three years for full recovery. We housed and cared for over 350 volunteers at the church, including Habitat for Humanity, The American Red Cross, and of course Baptist disaster relief teams.

We who were pastors of churches were grateful and yet weary for having to host those volunteers.

During this time, I had suffered two heart attacks; the second one, I was medevacked to Honolulu and placed in ICU eventually when I got stabled, they placed a stint in my heart. I was warned to take it easy for a couple of months and to exercise slowly until I got better.

When I got back to Kauai, once again the very first day I was criticized for not doing enough!! "Hey guys, I just had a heart attack and was told to take it easy for the next several months!" (Going to deaf ears.)

I was accused of hiding when I worked on drafting drawings to show the county officials the plans on the reconstruction of the church's educational building. (By state laws that was a requirement before any reconstruction could take place.) I was in and about the facilities measuring in plan site, how could I have been hiding? We had to get the drawings finished before volunteer construction teams came. I saved the church hundreds of dollars, while others had to pay for professional help from Honolulu costing them.

Empty Nest – The Biggest Battle of All – Last Move

After "Iniki", many had moved off island, those that stayed continued to experience many hardships. Before long trouble started brewing within the churches (division). With the stress of the recovery pastors including myself were targets for opportunist to stir up troubles for pastors and churches.

One of the Baptist relief leaders from the mainland USA had warned me that especially after disasters, opportunist will try to edge themselves into churches and even try to take over. I found this not only was going to happen in my church but it was happening in another church on the island.

About a couple of years later, a couple that had visited our church came to my office telling me they were about to be deported because their visas had expired. I helped them by supporting them financially by putting gas in the car they had, buying food for their family and even driving their children to school for several months. Trying to be compassionate because they were from another country.

They desired stay on the island to be with their family. I would work with the Baptist convention to get them a work visa to do language work in the island. As soon as the visas came in, they became very greedy wanting to take over the church, not doing language work at all. I should have seen it coming. (I was warned)

For a couple of years, they played havoc in the church. They had spread awful rumors about my wife and myself, these are the ones good friends told me:

"I was told by reliable sources that the pastor is gay."

"I heard the pastor say he hates Asians." (I married an Asian)

"Did you know the pastor is a womanizer."

"Hey, I just found out he served time in prison."
"That heart attack was faked so he could visit friends on Oahu."
I was told there was many other rumors spread.

The saddest of facts is that many of the people in the church believed the rumors. Including the two Baptist mission pastors. I became very distraught until God spoke to me giving me this:

Psalms 41

A few years after, we left the island we found out that the trouble maker and his family were deported for embezzlement. They were the opportunist I had been warned about. It happens in churches all over.

During this time our other two children would leave the nest. My middle daughter got married and moved to the mainland. My son went to the mainland for college at Oklahoma Baptist University. Just the two of us to fight the battle within the church. God in his way was going to move us for greater and better things.

My oldest, Stephanie, now in the Army in an engineering unit operating heavy equipment. She had been all over the world. She would have served in three combat tours and one humanitarian tour. (Somalia, Afghanistan, Liberia) In Liberia she helped missionaries in her spare time.

My middle child, Lani is a professional counselor and she donated a kidney to a total stranger. The youngest, my son, Ricky is a firefighter with the City and County of Honolulu. I have five wonderful grandchildren, all boys.

Big Things Happening for My Wife

In 1995 something spectacular happened to my wife. The Hawaii Baptist Convention selected her to represent Hawaii on the nominating committee of the Southern Baptist Convention. We were told she was the first Asian woman to serve on a committee with the convention.

We both flew to Nashville, staying in a fine hotel in downtown Nashville all expenses paid. While she attended meetings, I walked around the city visiting the local sites.

June of that year she went to the 1995 Southern Baptist Convention held in Atlanta Georgia. She was given the royal treatment from the WMU – Women's Missionary Organization.

At a historical event, she was on the platform when the convention made a special resolution.

RESOLUTION ON RACIAL RECONCILIATION ON THE 150TH ANNIVERSARY OF THE SOUTHERN BAPTIST CONVENTION

What an honor! Was I jealous...you bet I was? I had to stay back on Kauai and deal with some critical issues in the church.

While on Kauai, Dad would call, usually on a Saturday. One particular day he called; I could tell he was extremely upset about something that had happened to my brother. He shared that my brother needed money I told him I would send a check as soon as I could. My wife and I drained what was left in our savings to send to dad. I was going to give all that I had later, the situation with my brother had come to an end. It was empowering to know that Dad and my brother needed me. Financially, dad never helped me, I was always my own provider for my needs and with this event I would show him up. The next few years he continued to thank me for being generous at his time of need.

It was mid-September 1998, when a lump was found on my wife's breast. After being confirmed at the local hospital, we were advised to move to Oahu. The cancer she had was in both breast and the lymph nodes. A close friend that was a doctor told us to move; that the stress on her from the church, would not help, as well there would be better medical treatment would be in Honolulu.

She flew over and stayed with her mom while I began packing and getting ready for another move. I officially resigned the church.

I was shocked when some members of the church wanted me to donate our personal things, so the next pastor could use them. Even the curtains my mother-in-law bought in Honolulu, and was never reimbursed for from the insurance money after the hurricane.

I said, you can keep the furniture, I was going to keep the kitchen items and other things that I owned because most of it were heirlooms from years past within my family and gifts people had given me. Actually, the church had more than enough stuff to get the next pastor started. I took plenty of stuff to the Salvation Army Thrift shop that was mine.

Later, from a friend, I found out that that couple that had made so much trouble thought they would be the new pastor and take over everything including my personal belongings thinking all the items in the parsonage belonged to the church, including my library. I placed items in a small shipping container and shipped both our cars to Honolulu.

Over the years, I had a very large library; actually, too large. Shipping my library would be too expensive. A young man and his wife were planning entering the ministry. I gave them most all of my library, there were several volumes of commentaries and pastoral guides I gave them for helping me pack and clean the parsonage. It was so clean it could have passed a white glove inspection. Being overwhelmed, my desire was to be with my wife who was fighting cancer. God help us!

I had served there at that church for ten years and six months. I was told that was the longest term a pastor had at that church to that point.

For months we lived in a small bedroom in my wife's mother's home. It was a large home and by the time our container arrived, it made everything very crowded. Those were very stressful times for the both of us, with regular chemo and radiation treatments it was a day-to-day struggle. What made things worse for us at that time, for us there was little or no privacy. Then children from a cousin that lived down stairs were always in and out of our room. Weekend nights the house was filled with smoke and noise from the men in the family playing all night poker while my wife sick with cancer and chemo was trying to sleep in the next room. Real compassion yeah!

One day while at local mall, we ran into a former member that told us that people in the church said we had made up the cancer story to save face of us resigning the church and leaving the island. After ten years, no wonder the church had such a bad reputation within the Baptist convention. If someone told them the Easter Bunny was real but pastor Rick killed him, and ate him for dinner, they would have believed it.

Starting Again but On Oahu

Back now in Honolulu, the Baptist convention office provided opportunities to do pulpit supply. Later after doing a
supply pulpit located in Makaha close to the infamous surfing
beach. The group there wanted me to become their regular
pastor. The pay was small however, it was nice, but I had to find
more work to make ends meet. I took up substitute teaching
in public schools. The pay scale made the effort worthwhile.

My wife finally completed her teaching degree while going
through the cancer treatment. It was a struggle for both of
us. She graduated from the University of Hawaii with a BA
in special education and elementary teaching. Soon she was
teaching increasing much needed income. The struggle was
not yet over. In a period of a few months while out vehicles
were parked on the street, they were hit by a drunken driver
and totaled. In time we managed to secure a truck for me and
a car for my wife.

I was working two jobs, taking care of our living quarters,
cooking and cleaning while continuing pastoring at Makaha I
was on the verge of exhaustion when I began noticing some
severe discomfort that slowly but continually increased making
me feel weak. Eating became difficult.

My doctor, a fine loving Christian woman told me to see
a specialist. The x-rays would show that I had four very large
growths in my colon. This happened right after my wife's last
treatment for cancer.

Please God not this not now! – That was my plea. After surgery, they had removed 4 polyps, the size of a man's thumb. At
the doctor's office a couple of days later told me some great
news. He told me that two of the polyps were malignant.

But the good news was the fact that my own body's defense system had attacked the malignant cells; that I would not have to take chemo just take certain vitamins to boost my body's immune system. Thank you, heavenly Father.

The church at Makaha was meeting in a hotel in a large glass room next to the pool. I loved the people they were great especially after the struggles we had on Kauai. Unique with my compassion for surfing and I was baptizing folks in that famous surfing beach.

After a few years, the Hotel was sold and eventually the church disbanded. I wish we could have stayed longer; those folks were great.

Months later, we were approached by a Korean church to conduct English services. The church provided a meal for homeless people and provided English services in a small chapel within the church. For three years we were there. I even taught New Testament classes in a local Korean Seminary. Many came to the Lord. I had the opportunity to baptize a man in his mid-90's. We had to leave; the church had financial difficulties and could no longer support an English pastor.

Bucket List Time

In 2006, I had just turned 60 years of age when I started to focus on something I had wanted to do for years. My wife Kathy was working and her health great by then, mine was too so I started planning my great adventure of walking the Appalachian Trail from the start of the trail in Georgia to the border of Virginia. (About a 400-mile trek)

To be honest, I needed a break, I was about to burn out. The stress of caring for the home by doing all the cleaning, washing, cooking as well as holding two jobs. On top of that, my wife and I were having some very serious marital problems to the point we were going to counselors and considering divorce.

I believe the stress of us living in a house with multiple families certainly did not enhance our situation. I remember cooking a homemade dinner for my family. I had to pick up some bread at the store, when I came back, all the food was gone. The cousin's family downstairs had eaten it all.

I needed to get away. Growing up in those hills and mountains was something that I had missed. I had taken the family a few times to visit the area, especially the Smoky Mountains and Cherokee North Carolina, even white-water rafting.

In preparation I started walking up and down the hills on Oahu, increasing the distance each time. After the first month, I put weights in my backpack, increasing until I had the approximate weight I would be carrying. I studied maps of the A.T. and studied several scenic side trails. The planned time would be from early March through the end of May. Finally, I was ready. I took a flight directly to Atlanta.

Arriving in Atlanta making my way back to Cartersville, my cousin and her husband drove me up to the start of the trail. The trail starts in North Georgia. We had made a special stop in Jasper Georgia. I wanted to visit special people that had a powerful influence in my life, especially the spiritual aspect.

There in the cemetery in Jasper were those special people, that was Coreen and Bill. I had known them from my earliest childhood. I thanked God that they had been significant influences in my life and spiritual Pilgrimage.

I was dropped off at the start of the trail, late that afternoon.

My first few miles were rough. Yet, the smell of the forest and the sounds of creeks and brooks placed in my soul the wonders of the works of God. Truly it was peaceful even in the rain and sometimes snow. Within minutes, I had met people on the trail. I was told that time of year, many were starting the trail and that I would see all kinds of all ages.

Every 8 to 10 miles or so, on the trail there would be a simple shelter that could hold 10 to 20. I had a special Hammack I used sometimes if the shelters were full. At that time of year most of the folks on the trail were college students on spring break. With hiking many side trails, I figured I walked over 330 miles. The ground was hardly ever level, up and down up and down. I think the highest point I made was on Blood Mountain, about 4800 ft above sea level. That was tough, the air was thin at that altitude... or it was the fact that I was in my 60's.

During this time, I experienced three churches. Each one would be unique in its own way. It was common to stop in towns along the way to resupply and sometimes to wash clothes and bath your body. Some of us on the trail started getting ripe early.

Hiawasee, Georgia, was the first town I came off the trail to resupply and take care of a bad rash. I stayed in a cheap motel that was next door to a small church. I saw a man sweeping the porch of the church and asked him what kind of church was it. He told me it was and Anglican Church of England. He told me that the church was a mission church to small communities in the Blue Ridge Mountains.

I told him I was a Baptist minister and would like to attend the church, but all I had was hiking clothes. He told me there was no dress code for attendance. The next day was Sunday. Walking into the church, I notice the man that had been sweeping was the priest of the church. Trying not to be noticed I sat in the back pew when two ladies invited me to sit closer. At the end of the service, they had communion; the same two ladies pulled me out of my pew and invited me to partake.

The priest came and asked me if I would lead the Sunday school class, because he had to counsel someone. I did, the group was fantastic. Most of the time I was bombarded with questions about Hawaii. Years later I found the churches website – they were growing and the ministry programs had expanded.

The next church was the Baptist church in Franklin North Carolina. They had a very special ministry for hikers on the trail. They provided a full breakfast and a Bible to all the hikers. I sat with the pastor and had a great time of fellowship.

Everything was fine hiking the trail until I slipped off a mountain in a rain storm fracturing my foot. I managed to get to a highway and made my way back to Franklin N.C. where my cousin would come and take me back to Cartersville. I do wish I could have finished my plan.

The last church I attended was a small Baptist church in Cartersville after I had got off the trail with a fractured foot and was staying with the cousin that dropped me off at the trail. I went early and introduced myself to the pastor who gave me a long hug and welcome. I went to Sunday school. That day they had singing and testimonies. I loved it!

That was the end of that. God had his timing; I came back just four days before my father-in-law passed away at Tripler Army Hospital. I conducted his funeral. Being a retired Marine being in action in WWII, Korea, and 3 tours of Vietnam.

For years he would brag about being an atheist until his health drastically failed. While he was in Tripler Army hospital, I contacted a local pastor to visit him. The pastor was from Texas, at that time he was pastoring Mililani Baptist church. There at the hospital pastor Gene Phillips led my father-in-law to receive Christ.

My wife went to visit him giving him a Bible; reading the gospel of John, he told my wife, "I remember this when I was a child in vacation Bible school growing up in Texas.

I continued to fill in pulpits and do substitute teaching until turning 70 with full retirement drawing an income from the Baptist Annuity Plan that I had and Social Security.

For another couple of years, I did interim work in a small church in another denominations. After they called a pastor. I began a work with Micronesians getting them established within the local Baptist Convention. That year those Micronesians had a state record of baptisms. Truth is that they all were sprinkled as babies (Lutheran background in their islands) I conducted a seminar of the history and doctrine of baptism. At a park close to Waikiki, the entire adult group in the church was baptized in the ocean (no sprinkling).

From that time, we began visiting churches all over, not necessarily looking for a home church, until I discovered a Baptist church starter on the west side of Oahu. I visited one time and stayed with them for three years until they had to disbanded due to finances. We went to another Baptist church for a year and a few months conducting a Sunday school for adults. Soon we visited another church, to our surprise this church was affiliated with Southeastern University back in Florida. conducted home Bible study for over two years until the worldwide corona pandemic hit.

Bucket List for My Wife – Mission Trip

For years, my wife, Kathy had desired to go on a mission trip. Our doctor, fine young Christian woman, went on medical mission once a year. After inquiring, Kathy was allowed to go on the next medical mission trip to Miramar for three weeks. I was lonely while she was gone, but happy she could have her dream come true.

Other Big Battles - Surfing – Heart

Surfing was the center of my physical activities. I had learned the joy of body boarding (Boogie board). In my senior years, I could enjoy bigger waves, whereas long boarding bigger waves were just too much at my age. I body boarded with several senior guys and gals at the wall in Waikiki. We watched out for each other when the waves got really big.

In Waikiki when the waves were 5 feet and above, I would go out. Surfing the same area meant you get acquainted with those around you. All knew me simply as pastor Rick. Many that knew me that had to go to class or work would ask me to keep time for them.

One day a very scantily dressed girl paddled up to me. It was difficult for me not to stare. She asked. "Some of the guys told me you were a pastor." I acknowledged it was so.

For months when the South shore was up the girl would come up to me and asked questions about Christianity and the Bible. From May to September, this went on until the end of the summer swell season.

The new season of the south swell came in early May, waves were five feet plus. Out in the water, I heard a voice,

"Pastor Rick, Pastor Rick." I saw a local girl paddling towards me. She was wearing shorts and a long sleeve rash guard shirt. It was the girl from last season. "Pastor Rick, I got saved!" That was the sweetest sound that I heard that season. She told me that I had answered her questions and had become active in the church she was attending and was even on the praise team.

There were sad times finding out from time to time one of the seniors that body boarded with us had died. One season, several of my relatives passed including my father. One of my favorite celebrity friends that lived in the Diamondhead area had also passed; he would say to me very early in the morning," Hey pastor Rick." Jim was a fine man; we had a lot in common -Jim from North Alabama and me from North Georgia.

At times a rare swell would come into the south shore ranging from 10 to 16 feet. One day catching one of the big ones out on the 3rd reef it was a wild fast ride until the entire wave closed out keeping me underwater for a long time. That scared me. *"Maybe I need to stay with the smaller waves now that I am getting older.*

My surfing days would end abruptly that same season. It was January 2011 when a large swell was reported to come in the south shore. That was rare for the south shore in the winter. That day the swell did not come. Many times, like that when the surf was not up, with no surf exercising by walking Ala Moana Park was the next activity.

At a place called Magic Island, a sail boat had washed-up on a rock pile jetty. There were some men trying to unload items from the wreckage. I thought I would give them a hand.

I had climbed up to the top rock and somehow fell backwards about 10 feet landing on rocks in the shallow water. When I came to my senses there were several people around me. One a tourist was a Canadian medical doctor. I think I was knocked out because there was no recollection of the fall in my mind.

They helped me to my feet; my whole body was numb. I slowly stood to my feet. The doctor said that my head was bleeding badly. The group stayed with me until they thought I could handle myself. The doctor said he was going to stay with me until I got to my car.

He wanted to call 911, but I begged him not to. That was really stupid, if I had immediate treatment, in time I could be back in the water today. At home I could not manage to get out of the car. My daughter-in-law was home and helped me. Male pride, I thought it would wear off.

The next morning my entire right side of my body from my feet to my shoulders was that purple black horrible bruise color. Any movement was extremely painful.

Over the weeks the pain got worse. Finally, I let my ego go and had x-rays, cat scans and MRIs that indicated that my hip had multiple hairline fractures and had fractured my spine with bone chips embedded in the spinal cord and needed surgery.

Months later, they even found blood clots in the back of my skull. I should have gone to a doctor immediately after the accident. My surfing days were over. It was God' timing now with age and injuries other physical problems came up. I was getting old and my mind and body had been fighting it, I finally gave in. Read *2nd Corinthian 4: 16*

You Shall Know the Truth and the Truth Will Set You Free

A while back, I was blessed to have a couple of cousins from the mainland to visit us in Hawaii, Donna and Judy. I had so much fun with them. Just like others over the years we would show them the island and do all kinds of fun stuff.

One evening after dinner, we were all sitting at the table chatting away, when a thought come to me about my mother. I was going to ask the oldest cousin if she knew something about mom.

When I was in Florida spending a month to care for dad and getting his house ready to rent or sale. I spent time clearing out his attic. It was sad that he had multiple boxes of photos and papers that were coved with black mold due to a leak dad had in his roof. I had to discard them after I went through them carefully.

There were a few boxes that were good, without mold. I noticed one small shoe box was filled with letters and cards written to my mother. As I was reading them, I found an old letter from mom's youngest brother, Buddy. The date of the letter was from the mid 1940's.

In the letter her brother, Buddy, was apologizing that he was not there to help mom when she needed it the most. My mom and uncle Buddy were the youngest in the Smith family. He wrote in the letter that he should have been there to protect her from what had happened. The event was not recorded in the letter. I asked the visiting cousin if she knew what had happened.

To my shock, everything made sense when she told me a person, a distant relative in the family had sexually abused her and others in the family. To make it worse everyone knew what was going on.

The guilt of having to go through that had made mother mentally unstable and feeling shame and guilt, later causing her to drink. Especially, when I was born with that white hair and the family gossip on both sides appearing that I was not my father's child.

Upon hearing that, the understanding of what had happened to her made me see mom in a whole different light, erasing all the negative feeling towards her vanish. I cried off and on for days. That knowledge healed all the last of my negative feelings towards her that I held in my heart as long as I could remember. It was not her fault dealing with me when she had major issues within herself. Understanding someone is valuable in healing relationships.

Full Retirement – Watching Grandkids

Due to my physical condition now, I stayed home watching and caring for the grandkids taking them to school, picking them up. My son and his family lived with us in the same house. We were blessed. The house was like two houses joined. Six bedrooms, four baths two kitchens. The house sits high on a hill with a view of the South shore of Oahu and all of Pearl Harbor. This home was owned by my mother-in law. She gave it to my wife and son while she bought another home a few blocks away.

I will share in the next sections unique events in my life, they are not in any order, I write them as they come to mind. Time sequence is not as important as the stories. As I write these stories, remember that God moving in people's lives continues today just as it has throughout human history. Miracle still happens!

Man cannot limit God. God moves today in the lives of his children just as much, if not more than he did from the first churches establish long ago.

Read these stories with an open mind in hopes that it will increase your faith, and empower you to be used of God with whatever gifts and opportunities He gives you. These stories are not in any specific order.

SHORT STORIES
NEXT DOOR NEIGHBOR – 11:00 PM (1978)

Before we left Hawaii to move to the mainland for schooling, one of the teenagers next -door came to visit me late in the evening. When she came into the bedroom, I was laying on the bed in my underwear.

She was the piano player in her church and had always desired to attend a Christian college. She told us that her dad was not going to pay for her education in a Christian college and that she would have to go to the University of Hawaii or pay for her own schooling.

We had prayer for her asking God to provide a way. I told her to go ahead and attend the school in Hawaii, and she could take some basic courses until God opens the door. We also asked God to help us forget the petition in order that our faith would not waver.

That fall she came back to us with great news. It seems that she had an uncle that was a very successful businessman. He told the girl's family that he wanted to put her through college – any college of her choice.

She enrolled in a large Christian university in the mainland achieving a five-year nursing degree. Her miracle came for her and can for anyone, just have faith. Today, she is the executive nurse of a large conglomerate of hospitals in Hawaii.

James chapter 1.

Her answer came months later – you have to be patient with faith and accept the fact that God has his timing. Too often we expect immediate answers. That is because we live in an instant gratification society, everything is fast – fast food – instant entertainment – instant access to the world through the internet.

THE BIG ONE – THE BIGGEST MIRACLE EXPERIENCED (The unity of faith)

The big miracle came right after hurricane "Iniki" hit the island of Kauai. (1992) Things were bad, 98 percent of our island had sustained major damage. During this time, no power, limited contact outside the island, people were hurting all over.

One afternoon a worker from city hall located in Lihue Kauai. Asked me if I could come to a special meeting at 6:00pm. I told him I would be there. He told me he would meet me outside city hall. It had been just only a couple of weeks or so since "Iniki" hit Kauai.

I was met at the door, then escorted down to the basement. There was still no power, but the city hall had generators. There in the basement were all the city officials, about 15 or so, sitting in a simi circle in a dimly lit gathering. It looked spooky.

I am thinking, *"What did I do wrong now?"*

The mayor stood and addressed me, "Pastor Rick, you have been a blessing with the Baptist setting up the kitchen, you continue to serve your church and community allowing us to use the church's facilities. For training our police and firemen. We are here today to ask of you to pray for us."

Wait, a government is not supposed to be religious. But these were trying times for all of us and we all needed help.

I was told another hurricane was headed towards Hawaii. I was surprised. In that room were all the local officials in one accord wanting prayer for Hawaii and especially our island.

I said, "let us then pray." I asked God to spare the islands from the hurricane. I told Him we were all tired and stretched to our limits. I then asked Him to honor these officials for coming together in one accord to seek divine intervention. (I don't remember the exact words but, I know God honored those officials.)

The church and the parsonage were just a block down the street from city hall. It was about 7:00 am that morning when a member of that group came running up to my office window and said, "Pastor Rick, the hurricane turned away!" God honored the governing officials by seeking him for help.

1 Corinthians 1

Miracles are real, they are not just for way back in Biblical times. God wants you to experience all that He has for you, just have faith the size of a mustard seed.

GIRL ON THE BEACH

Some miracles may seem small, but they can have a big impact on people. This one happened on Kauai and Oahu.

Shortly after hurricane Iniki hit it was close to graduation time for the senior class. My daughter, Lani and several of her friends wanted to have a beach party. We had it a beach in Kapaa on the mid-east side of the island.

Noticing one of the high school girls walking by herself on the beach. I asked her, "What's wrong are you're alright" At that she opened up about how she looked thinking she will never find love.

I told her that anything God makes is beautiful. I mentioned to her that both in the animal and plant life that many things take time and effort to grow and change. I continued saying, *that will happen to you one day, I believe it.* She smiled, we hugged.

Several years later, after my wife and I had moved back to Honolulu, my daughter from Washington State came to visit. I remember it was Independence Day. That day we had many guests including special friends from Nashville, Bill and Genie. Bill was a piano player for the Statler Brothers and Genie was a backup singer for Dolly Pardon.

Several of my daughter's friends from Kauai came over to swim in our pool and have a party. I saw a girl standing by the pool. She was absolutely beautiful. I asked, *Who is that?* She shouted back, "Pastor don't you remember me and out talk on the beach. This was miracle. She believed that she could look and be a better person. She had lost weight and had married.

Please remember that small miracles are just as significant as the big ones.

I NEED ONE TOO (2020)

There are so many more, I would have to write another book, However, there was another miracle I experience was for me personally.

In the middle of the corona pandemic, I woke up one night, feeling like an elephant was stomping on my chest. I woke my wife up to take me to the emergency room. (My fourth heart attack)

There in the room they had me on an IV with medication to help with the situation.

I thought, this was the end, God did not need me in this world anymore. I felt a peace when I asked God to give me a sign. At that moment such a peace come over me, it seemed there were bright lights in the room almost angelic, I thought I was already in Heaven or about to enter heaven.

All of a sudden, a nurse came in speaking in a thick southern drawl. I spoke, "Where are you from?" She answered, "From Melbourne Florida."

I told her that I had lived there and that my father was the city manager there.

Then she said, "Was his name Watkins? I said yes," I think my dad and him were friends, my dad worked for the city of Melbourne." WOW, that was GOD! She stayed with me for a good while talking.

Two days later I am taking a treadmill (by medicine) test indicating I had severe blockage in the lower part of my heart. It was suggested that I do a procedure that would open up the area by using a balloon thing to open the vein or even place another stint in. If that did not work, I might have to have open heart surgery.

One week later, I was in the hospital getting the procedure when all that was there were shocked. The blockage disappeared before their eyes on the X-ray screen they did not have to do the procedure.

At the follow up with my cardiologist, he just threw his hands up in the air," Rick, I don't know what to tell you." Then shook his head when I said, "Would you call it a miracle?" His response was that I had the heart of a young 50-year-old man (I was 74 at that time) "Go and enjoy life with good health."

JESUS SAID, HE WHO COMES TO ME WILL I,
IN NO WAY CAST OUT!

I learned early how rejection had felt – Like Jesus, I would minister to any and all. I believe that the unconditional acceptance of others where they are, for the Christian it is an opportunity to be used.

It was back in the early 80s while I was still in college and pastoring a church, we decided to take a trip to see my parents for Christmas. I had one of my professors fill in for me. Melbourne only about an hour and a half away from Lakeland.

I decided I want to go to a special service advertised in the local Melbourne paper. We were late getting there and had to sit on a pew close to the back of the church. Others came in and filled the church.

The pastor was preaching on Revelation and was in the middle of the sermon when a man walked in all the way to the front of the church's pulpit. He bowed his head and folded his hands.

Immediately the pastor yelled at him and told him to get out he was interrupting his sermon.

The man slowly turned and walked out. I wanted to leave too but we were trapped in the middle of the pew. I thought to myself if something like that happens to me, I will stop and minister to whosoever needs it. Remembering how Jesus responded to interruptions. (Woman with the issue of blood – (recorded in 3 of the gospels)

A few weeks later it was Wednesday night at the church I was pastoring in Lakeland, rather than a prayer meeting it was a business meeting. We had just got started when a man came in walked down in front of the pulpit bowing his head.

I told the church, "I think we need to set aside our business meeting. I perceive this man need us." I called for the deacons to come up and pray with the man, before long the whole body of Christ there surrounded the man. (We had us a mini revival)

OH, WHAT OR WHO IS THAT!

It was 2003 when a Korean church hired me to conduct services for the homeless in a small upstairs chapel.

One Sunday a heard a loud commotion outside the chapel. The older Korean women were talking and shouting angerly. As I looked down the stairway, I saw a transvestite wearing women's clothing with a bad blond wig. He had been on a binge; I knew the look he had was one I grew up with in my home. Knowing he was sober, I had him sit with my family.

While singing the old hymns and old-fashioned preaching of a simple message, I noticed streams of tears coming down his face. The end of the service, I gave him a hug and thanked him for coming.

From there he told me he had just got out of the Navy. He then told me his dad was a preacher back in Oklahoma.

He continued to tell me the service had convicted him and that he was going home to make things right with his family and with God

I wonder if I had the attitude that some churches, denominations and pastors have, if he had come to those would the same thing have happened? I hope that it would have.

We have to ask the question, *what would Jesus do?* It is easy to do that around other Christians but what about those that many would consider undesirable?

HOW DARE YOUR LET NON-MEMBERS DO THAT (The gifts of music)

I had conducted many weddings while on Kauai. At one wedding I met and talked to a piano player, Rose. Our former piano player had moved to the mainland. I mentioned the fact we did not have a current player and if she might volunteer until we find one. Rose agreed.

She played for us on a regular basis when I got some comments from one of the members, *Why are we letting her play, did you know she plays in local night clubs?* (I ignored the comment)

One service during invitation, Rose stopped playing and came forward giving her heart to Christ. Later she told me her son was a youth worker in a church on the big island of Hawaii.

I called her son asking him if he would fly over to baptize his mother next Sunday. He did, that was so powerful, I don't think there was a dry eye in church that day.

One day a retired band teacher from the local high school on Kauai called and wanted to talk to me. "Sure, come on over"). His kids not only knew my kids, they often hung out together.

Tom came over to ask me if I would like to give an opportunity to former band members from the high school. There were not many opportunities for former band members to continue their skills in music. Tom asked if he could have them come and play in our worship services. Of course, I said and gave him the hymns we would do for that Sunday.

That worship service filled the sanctuary with sounds of brass, woodwinds, strings and a fantastic music leader, Tom.

We had many tourists to visit the worship, that day the house was packed. The hymns ended in applause and shouts. (Shout unto God with the voice of triumph). I was met by one very irate church member, "How dare you let none church members come into my church and do that. I responded, I always thought this was God's church? That made her furious.

Over the months ahead, the band not only continued but one by one some got saved and baptized. The church was growing fast. I caught that same lady one Sunday telling new people to find another church. The trouble with her and a couple of others continued.

A few years later I was called back to Kauai to conduct Tom's memorial. I will hear Tom play again one day.

The ten and a half years I served there; the church had become a focus of community activities. We had things from tutoring services for kids, Weight watchers, Police and fire training. And many more, but a few members hated that we were using the church facilities for the community and yet when we did some of those folks got saved and our focus in the community had a very positive view. In Biblical times the temple and synagogues were the center of community activities.

I paid the price the more I would open the facilities to the public the more problems I faced with a few of the old-time members even though these events brought people into the church resulting in salvation. This is a problem with many churches all over and within many denominations, I call it the *country club church* mentality... exclusive – for members only. I just don't find that in the teachings of Christ.

BE SURE YOUR SINS WILL FIND YOU OUT

Galatians 6: 7 Do not be deceived, God is not mocked; for whatever a man sows, that he will also reap. 8 For he who sows to his flesh will of the flesh reap corruption, but he who sows to the Spirit will of the Spirit reap everlasting life.

Years back I had a most unusual event happen to me. One afternoon I received a call from a local funeral home. I had presided over the years many services there. The director wanted me at the home to deal with a serious and very unique problem.

Arriving there, I saw him with a young attractive woman sitting on a pew in the chapel. The director took me into his office and explained the following problem:

A gentleman had died in a freak accident with the ambulance bringing him directly to the home.

"Rick, I have a big mess on my hands. The woman on the pew told me they had just been married. Before I could do anything with the body, I needed proof of the marriage. The woman showed me a license that was a fake, in Hawaii many con artists will fake wedding credentials to make a fast buck what was shown was only a copy of a certificate and not a license. "She told me they had just got married and were on their honeymoon when the accident happened."

He continued to tell me they had contacted his legal wife in another state. They were not divorced confirming the fake license the young woman had. He was waiting for the real wife to come to retrieve the man's ashes.

In the meantime, the young woman was requesting a simple service. (She was not informed the marriage she thought she had was illegal.) I had to tell her the truth. She told me she did not know that, but she had a deep love for the man she thought she had married. I agreed to do a simple service the next day.

Next day the service was held late in the afternoon, when the legal wife showed up. Before the service, I had informed the young woman of the legalities of the situation.

The real wife came out of the director's office with a bag of all the personal belongings of the deceased man, including, wallet, check books, jewelry and all of his personal belongings. The young woman was very upset. Even more so when the wife took the bag of ashes and flushed them down a toilet next to the chapel. (Lesson – don't cheat!)

A HOSPITAL MIRACLE THAT WAS STRANGE

(In the dark)

I was the on-call chaplain at the local hospital because I was the closest to the hospital. One evening I got a call that a couple had requested a chaplain.

It was about 3:30am. I stubble into my office and picked what I though was my prayer book. When I arrived at the hospital, I looked down to see that I had accidentally picked up my wedding manual rather than my prayer book. I thought to myself, I will just pray like a good Baptist minister would right from the heart.

I was ushered into the room when I saw an older man and woman on the bed. I asked them why did they request for me. Then I was told that over 50 years ago they had been married by a justice of the peace and had promised each other one day they would be married by a minister. I looked down at my wedding manual and thanked God for that wonderful mistake.

A doctor told me that time was critical that he would not last until daybreak. Because it was late and all the other patients were sleeping several of the staff entered the room to witness their wedding. When I finished, I stepped out of the room when the bride and groom kissed and all there applauded. Not even a couple of minutes the doctor stepped out and informed me the gentleman had passed. The lesson I learned that night, God can even use your mistakes and turn them to greatness.

A SPECIAL GROUP OF WONDERFUL PEOPLE

(Judge not less yea be judged...)

There was a time, I did some work with Micronesians at a local church. There was an influx of these people that were allowed to come to Hawaii. Many of them needed medical care. This happened due to the atomic bomb testing that happened years ago. In and around their islands. The locals viewed them as ignorant. (Only because they did not understand local, state, and federal laws.)

With these warm and simple loving people. I had the privilege to work with them setting up and training them to form their own church.

I had written a booklet on operating a church in the USA. I had helped them to understand state, city and federal laws.

I was honored when one of their men had my booklet translated into their own language. When they were equipped enough to be on their own. It was time to move on and let them thrive. The pastor of the congregation became the leader of Micronesian ministry with the Hawaii Baptist Convention.

During this time, I was overweight and my blood sugar was not that great. MY wife was still teaching at that time and my mornings were free. I decided to get some exercise and somehow get back in shape. I started daily walks in a large park a few miles from home.

One day I saw a young man sitting by himself with a backpack. We talked. I found out he was homeless. I asked him if he would take me to his campsite. There were eight others there at a site located in some thick brush under some shade trees. For the next several months I brought them food, toilet paper, plastic bags and such.

One day one of them said that I looked tired. I shared with them that I was going through some struggles, when to my surprise, one of them said, "let's pray for pastor Rick. I was so touched I cried. After that while I had good health, I continued to help homeless. Hawaii has a large number of homeless individuals as well as families.

My wife, while teaching in a local school, had found out that a couple of students and their family lived under a bridge that was close to the school. I went to see them and found out there were 14 altogether. Daily I brought them ice and food until they obtained housing. (Please note: of this group 4 adults had full time jobs – only adult that stayed in the camp was a 68-year-old grandmother who also watched a toddler while the rest of the children were in school.

MINISTERING TO HOMELESS

So many Christians I come across in local churches had a very different opinion of homeless people - roughnecks, drugees, low lives, bums, lazy, ex-cons. These people are not only were human beings, many of them had jobs and families, but could not afford the high prices of local rentals and government housing had a long waiting list. One day, God is going to judge us on our perspective of how we look at others – look at them with the eyes of Jesus and give them the same love and compassion as Jesus would. By the way the family of fourteen got housing.

My heart burst with pride when my son picked up their kids in that family to take them trick or treating on Halloween (all saints night).

SPECIAL PEOPLE THAT IMPACTED MY LIFE

Gifts can be anything God places in your life that would lift you up including the gifts of compassionate friends. There are many people in a person's life that can make a powerful difference, especially when things are difficult.

<u>Professor of philosophy – Dr. Milton H.</u> and his wife came to visit at one of our Sunday evening services. Usually, we did

some old gospel songs and times of testimonies and prayer. The very next Sunday they came to the morning service. At the end of the service Dr. Milton asked me if I could meet him the next morning for breakfast and that he had some things he wanted to discuss with me.

I was timid, I had heard he had debated some famous people and made mush out of them. Really, I was scared out of my wits thinking he was going to debate my sermons and teachings.

I arrived at the restaurant to find him already at a table. We ordered coffee and a light breakfast. While eating he began to share,

" Pastor, you have brought me back to days growing up in Oklahoma of good ole sawdust trail type of worship, singing, and preaching."

He continued to tell me he was dying of bone cancer that was beyond treatment. He was ready to go and see Jesus and his parents. The style of worship had brought joy to his heart.

Wow, I did not expect that response. A few months later his wife took him back to his home in the mainland where he passed into glory. He gave me the biggest pat on the back a preacher could ever get.

Dr. Herman and Rayberta Ray and the members of Waikiki Baptist Church and the Aloha Chapel Ministries (1971-1979).

(Learning of boldness to speak for God)

After a few weeks of membership at Waikiki Baptist. Dr. Ray encouraged me to take a vocal part in the hotel ministry by leading, singing and finally bringing the message.

From the moment I stepped into the church, it was like instant family. It was that church and its ministry that forged me into becoming as active Christian. Dr Ray would not let up giving me responsibilities and duties that instilled a bold desire to preach and teach the gospel. The best gift the Rays had was making people feel important. I named my middle daughter, Lani Rayberta.

(Learning how to treat adversaries.)

The sailboat builder I don't remember his name, he had spent a few Sundays with us on Kauai. He built high class sailboats. The time he attended our church we were in the middle of some severe church conflict (I mention previously). He took my wife and I out to dinner one night to talk to us giving us assurance and validation. He had shared his experiences with people that were trouble makers.

The timing was perfect we were on the verge of leaving at that time when he told us this: "Always remember this fact, the best revenge is to live well, live far above those that want to harm or destroy you and your ministry. Remember the Bible says, beware when men speak well of you. You don't want to fall into the trap of being a people pleaser – you want to be a God pleaser."

Today, I live daily thinking of those wonderful words of encouragement. Anytime trouble come in from others, I focus on living well and pleasing God.

(The gifts of evangelism)

Lloyd G. Harbor City Baptist

Lloyd was a unique individual. He worked as a lineman for the phone company. He had a speech impediment. Yet, that never bothered him or stopped him from leading folks to Christ. I look up to him as being one of the finest soul winners I have ever known. His technique was a one on one with people. He would build a relationship with them then share with them the gospel.

I went on visitation with him time after time. Spite his speech impediment, it never stopped him from sharing. I spent much time with him on visitations a great learning experience. He used a term I still use today, RELATIONSHIP EVANGELISM. Establish a relationship with someone that will take the investment of time and effort, then share the gospel with them.

By the way, he was a fantastic fisherman taking many fishing and leading many to Christ.

(Pride comes before a fall)

A man that made me swallow my pride It was about 1978 when I had to work late one Saturday evening. The next morning, I had promised that I would set up one of our hotel services and lead the singing at another service later that morning. The two hotels were the Holiday Inns, one to the far east of Waikiki and the other to the far west.

I was not in a great mood that day. Tired and frustration illuminating from work the night before made me a bit on edge. Arriving early in order to have coffee and a light breakfast, I was approached by an older man. "I was told you are in charge of the service at 8 am?" Yes, I will be there soon, it is only 7:30.

He asked me if he could do anything to help. The chairs were already set up. I told him in a closet close to the chairs he could pull the organ out, along with the pulpit.

In no time he finished, and asked me was there anything else? I told him to seat the guest when they start to arrive. The service only last about a half an hour. After the service I was taking to one of the guests when the older man asked me if there was something else? Simply, I told him. "Put everything back in the closet." That man was starting to get on my nerves.

I was already late for the other Holiday Inn; I was supposed to lead the singing. I ran towards my VW van, when the older gentleman yelled, where are we going next?

I told him." Listen I have to go all the way to the other end of Waikiki and I am not coming back here." Shocked by his response, "Don't worry that is where I am staying anyway." Speedily I drove to the other end and he and I rushed up the escalator to where the poolside service had started. Dr. Ray had just finished the singing when he wanted to do a special introduction. "Ladies and gentlemen, I want to introduce to a man that has been a great support for years in our ministry in the hotels of Waikiki." I am thinking to myself, "Please Dr. Ray don't blow up my ego balloon."

Then he announced, "Would all of you turn and meet Wallace Johnson, one of the founders of the Holiday Inns. I turned slowly to look at the older man when he said laughing, "You didn't know who I was did you?"

"I am so sorry please, so sorry." Glooming with embarrass-ment. His response," I was thrilled I could pull this off on you,

I had a great time." He continued, "If you are ever in Memphis, give me a call, you can even stay in my home.

Three Great Professors that extremely helped me to focus on ministry and personal guidance. (Gifts of encouragement) Dr. R. A professor of pastoral theology and practice, continued to advise and guide me in pastoring that first church in Lakeland while I was still a student. When the position of the church opened after the former pastor resigned, he gave me the best advice for a small struggling church:

a. You have to be bold; you have to lead. It is like a runaway bus going down a steep hill and no one wants to take the wheel – that is your job as pastor of a small church.
b. You have to clean up the mess former pastors have left in order for the church body to heal.
c. You must instill a vision for the church and a direction for the people to go. (Many times, in a small church people fight change)

I would sit with him discussing what I needed to be doing in the church. He would tell me stories of his first church how many times he had to take the bull by the horn to get things done.

I had several professors in seminary that became friends. Each of them came to Hawaii to visit after they retired. While a student, I took

One stayed an entire month on Kauai with wonderful times of conversing, especially the topic of growing up in a dysfunction home. Dr. D – professor of psychology and counseling.

He had written over 60 books on psychology. I learned much about the dynamics of dysfunctional families but what helped me the most was recognizing the various roles in such a family. Although many specialists have their own descriptions and titles of the role's families play, the primary roles usually fall into these categories:

The Addict – traumatic events led victims into negative behaviors linked to addictions resulting in mental issues.

The Enabler – the excuse maker great at hiding or not recognizing the seriousness of the addiction and its effect on the family.

The Scapegoat – take much of the blame often feels rejected

The clown – seeks to bring normalcy in the home making light of things

The Shining star – believing living perfection and guarding the family secrets will bring peace in the home.

These are distinct roles that are similar in psychology, however, he wanted me to write my own with descriptions so I would better understand the roles the members of my family played. These roles too often would carry well into people's adulthood even to retirement these roles can still exist or pop up unexpectedly.

My role is easy for me to recognize, (using my own terms for all of these)

<u>clown/rebel – scapegoat</u>. Clowning made friends outside the family; the rebel kicked in after becoming the scapegoat feeling like I had become the black sheep ostracized by most my relatives, competing for attention in the family (negative attention is better than none)

<u>Boss King enabler magician</u> – his word was law, but only to me. He holds the power over the house but, he becomes the magician vanishing when he is needed the most.

<u>Guard/hero</u> – Duty to guard the families' secrets of the horrors of family life - was the role model for others outside the family to see defending secrets at all cost the guard/hero was the only one from their perspective that held the family together.

<u>(The charmed one)</u> focus and attention always on their needs and wants even well into their adulthood – better described as the golden child protected at all cost, could do no wrong. Their mistakes and faults are overlooked

<u>The doer/caretaker roles</u> – almost non-existent

<u>The addict</u> – has no control has no self-esteem uses addictive behaviors and actions to draw any attention to themselves carrying hidden guilts

<u>The outside police</u> – family and family members outside the home and local friends that lay guilt trips on the scapegoat. "If only you would do such and such, this wouldn't happen."

<u>The Historians</u> – those in the extended family that see you as the irresponsible wild youth well into your adulthood, spite your success as an adult – even though you are a senior citizen, they still see you as the irresponsible child.

I thank God for those professors that helped me through my struggles with this issue

(The gift of generosity)

TEACHING AND PREACHING ON THE TITHE

Back in the mid-80s, I met a retired third grade teacher that told me about a challenge she would give to young couples to start them tithing to their churches.

Here is the plan she would propose to these couples." If you will tithe using this method, if God does not take care of your needs (not your wants -smokes – booze etc.), I will pay you back everything you paid. Here is the setup: A. you have to give an account of all that you have spent B. start by giving one percent of your gross the first month – two percent the second month – (all the way to ten percent in the tenth month. – . the funds have to go directly into the church. (Not charity organizations etc.) Then she said, "If God does not take care of your needs, I will pay you back every penny you paid into your church.

The challenge she made was based on Malachi chapter three. (Note this book, focuses about the time of the Messiah.)

She told me she has never had to pay anyone that took the challenge and that I should try it when I have a church to pastor.

Every church that I had been pastor of, I would preach on giving and tithing once a year. The title of the sermon was, "Ye Ought"

Matthew 23: 23 Woe unto you, scribes and Pharisees, hypocrites! for ye pay tithe of mint and anise and cummin, and have omitted the weightier [matters] of the law, judgment, mercy, and faith: **these ought ye to have** *done, and not to leave the other undone.*

I would preach that tithing came before the Law of Moses and in the Law of Moses. It also came with the prophets (Malachi)- which focused on the coming messiah. And in the New Testament. (Ye ought)

I would point out that many would use the cop-out scripture as an excuse as not to give or give very little rather than try faith.

2nd Corinthians 9: 7 Every man according as he purposeth in his heart, not grudgingly, or of necessity:

That is between them and God. The problem is they would lack to faith and trust in God to provide for their needs (not their wants)

Philp. 9:14 But my God shall supply all your needs according to his riches in glory by Christ Jesus.

I had many positive responses, even a letter sent by some tourist that came to Hawaii. In that letter they never were told about tithing in their church and as soon as they got back home, they started and were thankful for the message on tithing.

Another response was from a tourist from the mid-west. He waited until almost everyone had left the church. He came to me, red faced and angry, "Pastor, I hope you have a big savings account, my business is about to go bankrupt and I am going to take you up on that challenge." Before he left, he made sure he had my full name, address and phone number.

I was nervous a bit, but I knew if he was sincere that God would bless him. It would be a few months before I would hear from him again. One day he called on the church phone. At first, I did not know it was him, his tone of voice was totally different. "Pastor, I did what you said, I am in my third month and I am doing the full tithe now. My business has recovered. Don't ever stop teaching and preaching the tithe."

SOUL WINNING

(He that wins souls is wise) Waikiki Baptist had been a launching pad for winnings souls. Our group from the church conducted a lot of street ministry, as well as those that would attend the Open-Door Coffee House. (The Christian night club) The first person I had the opportunity to lead to the Lord was a Navy Submariner He had many questions. We sat under a palm tree where I shared with him, he received Christ.

I did not see him for over six months. He showed up at my wedding and gifted my wife and I with a beautiful tapestry of Christ. I found out that he was getting out of the Navy and contemplating going into the ministry.

I am totally convinced that every Christian should be able to talk to someone about how to become a Christian. I also believe every preacher, deacon, and board member of a church should not only know how but have in the past led someone to Christ.

I was shocked when about 30 years ago I was at a conference for pastors when the question was asked." Other than an invitation at the alter call, how many of you have actually led someone to Christ on a personal one on one experience. Out of about 40 pastors there, only three of us raised our hands.

Every time I have an opportunity to teach methods of soul winning, I get excited when people put it to practice. A few of years ago during a Bible study in my home, we had a group of about 12 to 16 people, when a did a simple presentation on how to use the Four Spiritual Laws.

A lady in her late 70's mentioned that a relative of hers was in Hospice and needed prayer. She continued to share that she did not know where he was spiritually.

I gave her two tracts of the Four Laws telling her just to read it to him and let him follow along until it comes to the sinner's prayer.

The next day she called my wife excited that he invited Christ into his heart. The next day, he went home to be with Jesus.

Sometimes I get upset with those that would put the extras; - you have to clean up your act before you come to Jesus (that is like saying you have to be healthy before you see a doctor or go to the hospital).

Worst, are those that want the crying, moaning and groaning approach needing to make a public display (Oldtimers used to call it *the big show of repentance*).

I like the four spiritual laws, because it was how I got saved and how I have used it over the years. It is simple, does not use churchly language, and has a great, but easy follow up plan, and yes it does mention the need for repentance! I also like to use the Roman road in the tenth chapter of Romans.

TAKING TRIPS BACK TO THE MAINLAND

In 2003 I took a long vacation with my family. My middle daughter was married and brought her family; my son came as well. My older daughter was in the military and could not make it.

The focus of the trip was first, to bury my dad in Dalton and then attend the Smith/Middleton family reunion, mom' side of the family.

We did a lot of sightseeing in the north Georgia mountains. We stayed in a motel in Dalton as our base.

One of the activities we chose to do was to go white water rafting on the Ocoee River. In the 1996 Olympics that was the river where they did the kayak competition.

We had been down the river several times in the past. However, that day with hard rains up the river made the classification level higher than normal. My wife, son, son-in-law, and myself were in the same raft with our guide and two others.

Things were fine until we went over a large waterfall that caused the raft to flip over. I went under and got caught in a strong undercurrent that pushed my left leg into a rock formation that wedged the leg underwater. Holding my breath as long as I could, I asked God not to have our trip spoiled with me drowning.

I passed out and regained consciousness about a hundred yards down the river. I was picked up by another raft comforting to my family that I had made it.

I would be scraped and bruised from my ankle up to my groin. But blessed. That was God.

CLASS REUNION - KATRINA - AND ANOTHER MIRACLE

In 2005, I had to opportunity to attend my high school 40th reunion. I was excited to see those wonderful friends of my youth. Even though we were old, we danced to those wonderful songs of the 60's until we were exhausted, we would rest a few numbers then back out again. I stayed with my brother and his wife in Melbourne. I did take time to visit Margret Clark, she had been there for me in the critical times in my life helping me on my spiritual pilgrimage. We had lunch together in one of our favorite places to eat that had good ole BBQ ribs with homemade sauce...

After the reunion, I was eager to visit my sister in Slidell, Louisiana. The hurricane Katrina had hit the coast causing major damage, death, and major destruction. Her house and been flooded up to the ceiling. Even though she had survived, I had to see how she was doing in order to have peace about it.

I stayed a couple of days; she gave me the tour of the area. I also did some clean-up. She was blessed, a friend had loaned their travel trailer for her to stay in. my stay was short, I wanted to head out and do a quick visit of my old stomping grounds in Panama City before I had to fly back to Hawaii.

It was midafternoon when I arrived in Panama City. I drove by to look at the home we used to live in. I noticed the house of that cute girl that gave me my first kiss, wondering if her parents still lived there.

I knocked on their door, her parents were still there, another reunion. Those fine folks kept me involved in that little Methodist church. To my surprise, they called that gal, she was in town. Hearing that I was at her parents' house she hurried right over.

She had become a medical missionary for years in the mountains of Haiti, until she retired. Unique, that we had both wound up in the ministry. I had kept memories of that little Methodist church she invited me to.

I asked if they knew anything about the Nealy family. I was told the older sister still lived in the same house with her husband from when my family moved. I knew exactly where it was and drove over there, to her house. To see her and her husband.

I knocked on the door, a young man opened it, I saw her sitting at her dining room table weeping bitterly. "Who are you and what do you want." When I told the young man who I was, I heard Pat yell, "Rick, what are you doing here?"

I told her of my reunion and trip to visit my sister and the strong desire to visit Panama City one more time.

Pat told me that her only son had passed away and they were getting ready to do a burial of his ashes at a place where they went scuba diving over the years. Pat had known that I was a minister and asked me if I would do the memorial and that my being there at the right time, I would represent the friendship of our families since before Pat and I were born. I said, "Of course." We hugged, and laughed recalling the good ole days of our lives together, and memories of the past. She said it was a miracle I showed up right before they were to go out on the boat. A few years later Pat and her husband went to be with Jesus.

I LOVE TEACHING – TEACHING IS MY FAVORITE GIFT FROM GOD

Over the years in ministry as I look back, I believe teaching the BIBLE has been one of the most powerful tools. I have to include my wife; she too is a great teacher.

I have taught a wide variety of programs of the SBC – Experiencing God – Making Peace with your Past – Church History and others. I designed a program catering to the needs of new Christians and those that are contemplating the Christian faith.

I have found the most powerful of teachings, is to establish a foundation in a simple system that God had given me years ago, and it works just as good in today's world as it did when I started. I called the program – Beginnings.

A. Introduction to scripture – a brief summary of all the books looking at key items of common people.
B. Biblical doctrines: Faith, Sin, redemption, church, etc.
C. Church history from Acts to present time highlights of church growth through missions and how the different denominations formed
D. Finally going over the plan of salvation

It normally takes about a year to do this in a one-hour Sunday school class setting. At the end, students are encouraged to attend regular classes within the church. (Please note – the only book I have students to use, is their Bible with a guideline handout.)

I do not use books written by Christians unless they focus directly on the Bible, my focus is to train them to get answers from their own Bibles and depend on that. Then they can read those books – the problem develops when people quote and base their beliefs and studies more in those books that are more from the best sellers list than directly from the Bible.

I have taught in evening seminars with two-hour sessions. I have been blessed how this has strengthened people and has given new Christians a strong foundation.

One of the most unique results came from a young man, Mike. He and his wife joined my class one Sunday morning. At that time, we had about 10 to 12 students, all ages.

Immediately, Mike shared that he was an atheist and was only there to support his wife. I told Mike *it was fine*, I continued to tell him to be free to ask questions and that my answers and opinions would be based on scripture. From that time, they never missed a class.

It was common that after a year of completing the course, students would move on to a regular class in Sunday school. It was time for Mike and his wife to move on to other classes when Mike said, "I want to do this again for one more year." I told him that was fine.

A few months later, I got a call from Mike at 6 AM on a Sunday morning in the spring. Mike knew I was already up because I had to set up for the 7am service. I answered, "Hey Mike are you all right." There was a pause when I got a strange answer, "I am in the Lord's army pastor" "What do you mean Mike?" Then Mike told me that the class had answers all the questions he had, and he invited Christ to come into his heart and wanted me to baptize him. God did that!

THE CANADIAN AND THE CUBAN

One time, I had a lovely couple come to my Beginnings class. The gentleman was from Canada and his wife was from Cuba. They had been sailing around the world on their sailboat. They docked in Kauai; the engine on their boat had gone out and were waiting for parts to fix the problem. There was no hurry and would wind up staying a couple of months.

The first class, they did not have a Bible, I gave them a paper-back Bible that we usually give out. The wife asked me a question wanting to know if the church had Spanish Bibles.

I was shocked when she told us that new Bibles were outlawed in Cuba, and that you could only be allowed to keep a family Bible. She continued to tell us those old Bibles were so worn out, they copied scripture on pieces of paper.

I mentioned that I had to fly to Honolulu for a meeting and that I would pick up a Hispanic Bible for her. In Honolulu, I found a Hispanic/English Bible and brought it back to Kauai.

That Sunday we started the Beginnings class with a special presentation giving the Cuban lady that special Bible.

Immediately she began reading the third chapter of John's gospel out loud crying with tears streaming down her face. We all were so touched by this powerful scene; we all were weeping. That moment for all of us was powerful, we all felt the power of God' presence there that day.

The next week, the Cuban lady gave me a special gift. Somehow, she had found out on occasions, I like to enjoy and fine quality cigar. Several members of the church would gift fine cigars for birthday gifts. That next Sunday I was given one of the finest customed rolled Cuban cigars. It would cost me well over fifty dollars if I were to buy one at a specialty shop. Each week I would get another cigar until they left the island.

TRIPS ARE GETTING HARD BUT FORGED MEMORIES

It was the summer of 2014 a family trip was taken. We met up with my son and his family at Disney World, from there traveled to Louisiana to spend Independence Day with my sister.

Fireworks were legal there; we all had a blast. Stephanie, my daughter met us there. We did all the tourist stuff in New Orleans. I wanted to go to the World War II Museum, but my sister told me the area was dangerous to go and park your car. I was greatly disappointed.

From there we went northward into Georgia there we panned for gold and saw Stone Mountain. My son his wife and his son went to a Braves game in Atlanta. On to North Carolina where we went gem hunting and visited Cherokee NC. On to Tennessee at Gatlinburg and to It was fun, but crowded. The best part was watching the grandkids as this trip was an exciting adventure for them.

It was so much fun. It was sad when the trip was over. It was very difficult for me on that trip due to the injuries I sustained in 2011 with my back and hip. Traveling was getting difficult and at times extremely painful.

My wife and I flew to Vancouver Washington to spend time with my other daughter Lani. My stay was short and I wanted to get back to Hawaii. I was also getting low on my pain medication. My wife stayed there a while longer.

That year, several friends and relatives noticed that I had developed a dark spot on the right nostril of my nose. After putting it off, I made an appointment with my dermatologist. After taking samples for testing, it had turned out to be an aggressive form of skin cancer.

I was referred to a surgeon to cut the cancer out. After multiple surgeries I had 47 stiches to rebuild the right lower half of my face. As always, I would minister to staff with prayer. The procedure would take me through several surgeries. (One about every two weeks) My last day with the doctor and staff, we all had a big group hug and prayer.

My problem was the fact I had spent years of surfing and lifeguard duties very seldom using sun block lotions. I should have been much more careful. Late lesson but I pass this item to those that might need the lesson.

MAYBE MY LAST JOURNEY HOME

In time, I would take what I considered to be my last trip back to family and my roots. Health issues multiplied now in my 70's.

It was just after Christmas of 2018; I had found out that my brother in Florida had a rare form of leukemia. I knew I had to go and see him even if my own heath was failing. I also knew this might be my last trip and I wanted to spend time in the deep south that I loved so much. When your roots grow deep for hundreds of years, it pains to think about it. However, though Hawaii has been home for over half my life, Yet, I feel more at home here in my beloved south, good ole Dixie.

Years of service to God in Hawaii sound great, however missing blood family was difficult. I missed them so much – weddings, funerals and family reunions. Facebook was a good way to keep up with family.

Many that I knew from childhood into middle aged had already gone home to be with Jesus. My family of the good ole days was quickly vanishing. Even visiting some of the old-time survivors of my family was saddened by the fact we were all well into our senior years, deep down knowing that our time was short. I was going back for one more time, maybe to say farewell until we meet again with Jesus.

Rather than flying directly to Florida I would fly to and from Nashville, rent a car and drive slowly through memory lane. I had notified family members that I would like to see them.

I took my time and drove from Nashville, down to Titusville Florida. I passed and stopped by many places that were focal points of familiar memories past. I did drive much of the old roads rather than intrastate highways.

St. Augustine was a favorite place in Florida. I could not go through the roads I desired because of construction and repaving activities in the area.

To my surprise, going through Daytona Beach, it was motorcycle week. It was a slow wonderful ride through the area. Most of the bikers were my age, they might could have called it "Boomer Bike Week".

As I went from town to town, I noticed that many stores and malls that used to be thriving at one time, were permanently closed.

It was late afternoon that I pulled up to my brother's home. For the next few days, he and his wife were great host. I enjoyed seeing Titusville. Across the Indian River you could see the old vertical assembly building. I was driven to an air museum that was fantastic to see vintage aircraft.

Later in the week an auto show in one of the local parks where I linked up with a classmate of mine, Judy.

Judy invited me to a new church that she had been attending off and on. That Sunday, I met her at a local YMCA building where the church was meeting.

When I arrived one of the early services was over. I noticed an extreme wide variety of people – old retired folks – young folks -young families. Some were dressed what some in the south would consider to be regular going to Sunday meetin' clothes. Others were wearing very casual, warm Florida day clothes. And finally, some looked like they had just come from motorcycle week in Daytona. There were also a variety of ethnic groups, Asians, black, Hispanic, and others it was hard to tell what they were.

I thought, this is great, this is what church is supposed to be like. Judy was not there yet so I looked for someone to give me information about this unique church.

I found a young man named Brad and introduced myself. Brad was bald, muscular with tattoos all over. I asked him if he could introduce me to the pastor, I had all kinds of question I wanted to ask. Clearing his throat, Brad said, "I am the pastor." My next question on my mind, "What kind or what denomination is this church, it looks like it might be Pentecostal or Four Square. Brad answers with a big grin, "Oh, we are Southern Baptist." I almost fainted. By that time Judy walked in.

I found out that this type of church in several denominations was spreading all over the South. Today, each Sunday, I go online to hear Pastor Brad or one of the other pastors speak at the Titusville Florida church.

Early the next morning before daybreak I was ready to leave headed back to Georgia, Alabama, and finally Nashville Tennessee. I hugged my brother and had a quick prayer for Jesus to heal him. Then got on the road I cried and prayed for several miles knowing I would not see my brother in this again in this world.

After bypassing Atlanta, I drove the backroads to Cartersville staying with my second cousin Donna. Cartersville, even driving by our home dad built on Cherokee Street. I stayed a couple of days. I had some business at the courthouse, I owned some property and was getting ready to sell it.

I had contacted some special people I had to see. My Classmates and their mom, Margret Clark, that wonderful lady that had such an impact on my life. They all had moved up to those beautiful Georgia foothills.

We met for lunch at a hole in the wall type restaurant on an old country road. Nancy and Dee talked much with my cousin Donna. I spent my time talking to Margret.

Margret said to me," Oh Rick, you have done so much for the Lord, I have not done anything significant for Him." I told Margret, all that God has had me to do is because of her, she planted the seed. We both will reap the benefits of the harvest. We hugged and cried. That was the last time I saw her on this earth.

The next day, I drove up to Calhoun to have lunch with some more cousins. It was like a small family reunion. I really needed that. Afterwards, I headed out for Dalton.

On the way to Dalton, I saw a sign that revealed a museum had been constructed at the old Cherokee capital. This was also where the Trail of tears had started sending most of the Cherokee to Oklahoma in the middle of winter. I had a short visit; the place was fantastic. I wished I had more time to stay there.

I drove old Dixie Highway 41 into Dalton and stayed with my sister/cousin Jan. The next day, I was to meet up with the Watkins clan to have lunch at an all you can eat cafeteria. That was like another small family reunion. It had been so long; I did not recognize most of them. I heard one of them mention, "He looks like a Watkins now with that grey hair. That was great we must have stayed there and talked for several hours.

Deep in my heart, I had missed out on my southern family's life, and yet our hope in Christ would give us all an eternal family reunion.

The next morning, I would say goodbye to my family, mom and dad, J.L., Maude, Mark, all the Watkins there at the Dalton cemetery

I drove my rental car up to Dug Gap. The old path had turned into a paved road going over to the other side of the mountain. Gazing back towards Dalton then southward towards Calhoun and Cartersville. I knew this might be the last time I would view the home of my birth and childhood. With a lump in my throat, I headed towards Huntsville to see another cousin, Judy.

Another mini family reunion as she invited a bunch of the relatives over for dinner. I was blessed to see her in an Easter presentation at her church.

The next morning, I left early, headed back to Nashville to get a flight back to Hawaii. I still took the old back roads all the way into Nashville.

Like many baby boomers, I longed for the good times and good ole days, but realizing we can live in the past or even try to go there. It was time for me to let it go, age was creeping up on me faster than I had imagined.

As I mentioned with health problems, I will probably never go back. My life is filled with my own family, kids and grandkids. I will try to make wonderful memories for them. Like we baby boomers, they have to make their own memories and I want to be a part of theirs.

Be blessed, believe with miracles, believe God has a plan for you, believe in his word (the Bible), believe you can do all things through Christ!

PASTOR RICK

CPSIA information can be obtained
at www.ICGtesting.com
Printed in the USA
LVHW020425020622
720196LV00014B/1046